WHAT *the*
PSALMIST
IS
SAYING
TO YOU
TODAY

PETER
WALLACE

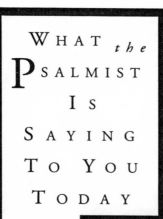

What *the* Psalmist Is Saying To You Today

Peter Wallace

THOMAS NELSON PUBLISHERS
Nashville • Atlanta • London • Vancouver

Published in Nashville, Tennessee, by Thomas Nelson, Inc.,
Publishers, and distributed in Canada by Word Communica-
tions, Ltd., Richmond, British Columbia.

Unless otherwise noted, scripture quotations noted CEV are
from the Contemporary English Version. Copyright © 1991,
American Bible Society.

Scripture quotations noted NKJV are from THE NEW KING
JAMES VERSION. Copyright © 1979, 1980, 1982, Thomas
Nelson, Inc., Publishers.

Library of Congress Cataloging-in-Publication Data

Wallace, Peter, 1954–
    What the Psalmist is saying to you today / Peter Wallace.
      p.   cm.
    ISBN 0-8407-9203-4 (pbk.)
    1. Bible. O.T. Psalms—Meditations. 2. Devotional calendars.
I. Title.
BS1430.4.W35   1995
223'.206—dc20   94–26947
                                      CIP

Printed in the United States of America.

1 2 3 4 5 6—00 99 98 97 96 95

For Alan, Cary, David, Dean, Jonathan, Jon, Ken, Wesley, and many other friends who have enriched my life beyond measure

INTRODUCTION

There are any number of devotional books available today. I hope this is unlike any of them.

My intention is that you not simply read it but use it as the basis for your meditations. I hope it becomes for you a doorway into the presence of your heavenly Father, who welcomes you and delights in your spending time with Him. And a springboard to launch your mind and catapult your heart into personal meditation and communion with the Lord.

What the Psalmist Is Saying to You Today is part of a series of daily reading collections designed to be flexible and interactive. The format enables you to follow along as you feel most comfortable, and it encourages you to be open to the Spirit's leading in order to find the truth you need at the moment you read it.

There are at least three ways you can read this book.

1. *You can read it a page at a time, a day at a time.* Each page is marked with the number of the day. You can start out with Day 1 on January 1 and finish up with Day 366 on December 31 (there's an

extra reading included for leap years). Of course, this is the traditional way of reading devotional books. And you may find it most convenient for you. But I would also urge you to consider one of a couple of alternative ways.

2. *Pray first, asking the Lord to direct your reading.* Then flip the book open to a page and read it. Or scan the verses to find one that hits you where you are. You may find you need to read two pages or even three at one sitting to find the one that speaks loudest to you in your need at the moment.

3. A Subject Index is located in the back of the book to help you find a reading that focuses on a particular concept. So if you're feeling lonely or confused, or if you want some insight on worship or encouragement, *look up these words and select a reading* that focuses on them. In this way your daily reading focuses on something relevant in your life at the moment.

You may think of yet another way to use the book. I hope you do because my goal is to encourage you to hear the psalmists' words as though for the first time. To hear them as though they were spoken directly to you. And to respond to them personally.

To this end, I encourage you to begin your time every day in prayer, to ask God to open your heart and mind to His insight and His will. Then read the page you've selected. Record your thoughts and prayers in a journal. Let the reading launch your meditation on the psalmists' words, focusing on how they can be reflected in your life today. Then follow with a time of prayer, asking God to help you respond in whatever way He wills.

This isn't a devotional book; it's a workbook. The comments I've included are designed to prod your heart and mind. I hope you will use this book to help you think and work through your struggles and frustrations in life. Let it be a guide to peace and serenity with your God.

If you benefit from using *What the Psalmist Is Saying to You Today*, consider reading the companion volumes as well—*What Jesus Is Saying to You Today* and *What God Is Saying to You Today*.

I would like to express my heartfelt appreciation to the special people in my life today who have contributed to my thinking and who challenge me to walk the path toward spiritual health and wholeness. They include my wife, Bonnie, my children Meredith and Matthew, my pastor, Gray Temple, Jr., Dr. Fred Hall, Harold McRae, Larry Smith, and my close friends Cary McNeal, Kenneth King, Jonathan Franz, Alan Charters, Dean Picha, Jonathan Golden, David Hodge, Wesley Greer, and many other wise men with whom I work and live and play and worship. All are precious to me beyond words.

May God open your eyes through the reading of these words from the book of Psalms. And may my comments not get in His way or yours.

—Peter Wallace
Stone Mountain, Georgia

DAY 1

God blesses those people who refuse evil advice and won't follow sinners or join in sneering at God. Instead, the Law of the LORD makes them happy, and they think about it day and night.

—Psalm 1:1–2

Consider this an invitation. It's an invitation to a life of delight rather than drudgery. Of light rather than darkness. Of positives rather than negatives. Of wisdom rather than emptiness. Of humor rather than bitterness. Of good rather than bad.

That kind of life, the psalmist explains, comes only from the Lord. And when you meditate on and delight in His Word, you will be rewarded.

It's not a matter of picking and choosing, here and there, whenever you like. It's a matter of immersion. Of soaking in the truth of God day and night.

By picking up this volume, you've taken a first step toward this delightful way of life because it will encourage you to read and wrestle with the Word of the Lord.

They are like trees growing beside a stream, trees
that produce fruit in season and always have leaves.
Those people succeed in everything they do.

—Psalm 1:3

Picture mature gnarled trees. Their limbs wide
and thick with leaves and loaded with fruit.
Standing strong by a stream rushing with life,
water spilling and splashing over the rocks.

The trees aren't going anywhere. They're doing
what the Creator intended for them to do: produce fruit and oxygen and shade and habitats
and mulch and seeds and delight and so much
more.

They're strong, firm, confident, and fruitful.
And you could be like them.

Note the key: People who delight in God's
Word and His will are like the trees. The source
of the fruitfulness is a living, active relationship
with God and His Word.

Why do the nations plot, and why do their people make useless plans?

—Psalm 2:1

Take a look at this morning's paper, and you may be tempted to quote this verse. It's been the story of planet earth for generations.

And in this case, the cause was utterly fruitless: "The kings of this earth have all joined together to turn against the LORD and his chosen one" (Ps. 2:2). The simpleminded leaders of the world, thinking they could overcome the Messiah and God Himself, plotted against them.

Humanity, it seems, has never lacked a high regard for itself. The race has always assumed it knows best how to run things—from the days of the Garden of Eden onward. But it's all useless.

In the face of this, God extends a compassionate hand of acceptance. He opens His heart to any who would come to Him in humble obedience.

DAY 4

I will tell the promise that the LORD made to me: "You are my son, because today I have become your father. Ask me for the nations, and every nation on earth will belong to you."

—Psalm 2:7–8

This is a word of God recognizing the authority of His Son, whom we know as Jesus, over the entire world. The Son of God owns the nations. They are His forever. He possesses everything, even to the ends of the earth.

Jesus is in authority over all for all time. He reigns indeed.

Now read the verses again. How real do they seem in your life? Is Jesus the Lord truly reigning in your soul?

The Son of God must be invited in personally to rule over your life. And when He takes possession of your soul at your invitation, He brings with Him His peace, His confidence, and His strength. The Lord reigns. Let Him reign in your life today.

JANUARY 4

DAY 5

Kiss the Son, lest He be angry, And you perish in the way, When His wrath is kindled but a little. Blessed are all those who put their trust in Him.

—Psalm 2:12 NKJV

There's a side of the Son of God you really don't want to see: His righteous anger. His hatred toward sin. His wrath toward ungodliness.

The psalmist encourages you to take another route: Trust Him. Place your confidence in Him. Let your soul rest in His hands.

Kiss the Son. In the psalmist's day, kissing one in authority indicated submission. It's a meaningful way of paying homage to the king. And that's a beautiful picture of putting yourself under the loving authority of your Lord, Jesus Christ.

Blessed are those who kiss the Son of God, the psalmist says. For they will experience His joy, His support, and His peace. And they will be spared His anger and wrath. Forever.

DAY 6

But you are my shield, and you give me victory and
great honor.

—Psalm 3:3

Surrounded by enemies, tormented by fear,
weakened by attacks. That was David's predicament. And today, you may experience similar
feelings.

In David's case, not only had the whole nation
under his authority turned against him, but so
had his own son, Absalom. David wrote this particular psalm after having fled for his life. And
yet, in the midst of that personal turmoil, he
could utter these words of comfort and encouragement.

God is a shield of protection in the battles of
life. He brings the victory.

That's the same God you love today. The One
who loves you, too.

I pray to you, and you answer from your sacred hill. I sleep and wake up refreshed because you, LORD, protect me.

—Psalm 3:4–5

The Lord God has big ears. Especially when He hears one of His children cry out in pain and fear.

David did. His son had betrayed him. The duped nation had turned against him. And he had run for his life.

The pain was unbearable. He cried out, and God heard him. As a result, he lay down. He slept. And he awoke, safe and sound. The Lord gave him the strength and comfort he needed to survive emotionally.

In times of emotional tumult, you may find it hard to let go. Sleep is impossible. Unless you, like David, can cry out to the Lord and let out all the pain and fear and doubt and disappointment. He hears. And understands. And then moves in mysterious and powerful ways.

The LORD has chosen everyone who is faithful to be his very own, and he answers my prayers.

—Psalm 4:3

To make a very basic distinction, there are two kinds of people in the world. First, there are those who love foolish things and seek what is worthless (v. 2). That is, those who focus their affections on anything other than the living God. And second, there are those whom the Lord has chosen, in other words, the faithful. Those whose lives are sourced in God and grounded on His Word.

Everyone must choose sides. But the psalmist says the choice is rather easy. Choosing God means He will answer when you pray to Him because you're His. And the truth is, nothing else out there can hear your cry. When all is said and done, the alternative to choosing God is choosing aloneness.

Have you already made your choice? Is that choice apparent in your life? Maybe it's a good day to call out to God.

Be angry, and do not sin. Meditate within your heart on your bed, and be still. Selah.

—*Psalm 4:4 NKJV*

When your life reaches the boiling point, it's easy to explode, to let all that pent-up emotion shoot out like shrapnel, potentially wounding others in its path.

God says when your life is filled with distress and disappointment, building anger, that's understandable. It's human to be angry. So He gives you permission: "Be angry." Recognize it, and deal with it.

How should you deal with it? Negatively, don't sin. Don't express your anger in a way that could hurt yourself or others. Positively, meditate. Rest. Take a break. Think it through. Pray about it. Be still. Be angry, but be still.

You move from anger to stillness through active meditation. Find out from God what to do to change the situation—or to change your heart.

DAY 10

I can lie down and sleep soundly because you, LORD, will keep me safe.

—Psalm 4:8

Sleepless nights. Tossing and turning. Fear, anxiety, and dread consume you. Your mind races uncontrollably.

You try everything to make it stop. But forcing it only makes it worse. Your brain screams for relief; your body aches with exhaustion. And finally, you pray this verse. Over and over if need be. Because it's a promise to those who trust in God. For He alone is able to protect and provide. Only He can offer you the care and comfort that you crave.

It worked for King David. At the nadir of his life, running away in fear from his son, he turned to his God in trust. And he slept in peace. Because he knew God would keep him safe.

Can you trust God that much today? He is able. He is willing. And He is waiting to hold you in His strong, comforting arms.

Each morning you listen to my prayer, as I bring my requests to you and wait for your reply.

—Psalm 5:3

What do you do when you wake up in the morning?

Rub your eyes and try to remember what day it is? Lie drowsily until you realize all the problems you'll have to confront today? Or do you pray? Or just look to the Lord?

David tells his Lord that he will turn to Him, talk to Him, and wait for His reply. First thing in the morning.

When do you get around to turning your day over to God? Try this. Tonight, write this verse on a card. Put it beside your bed. Tomorrow, when you wake up, remember David's example.

Tell God about your fears in the day ahead and the things you're looking forward to. Thank Him for being there with you and hearing you.

DAY 12

Because of your great mercy, I come to your house,
LORD, and I am filled with wonder as I bow down
to worship at your holy temple.

—Psalm 5:7

David made a choice that would unalterably
mark his life. He chose to enter the house of
God. He chose to take his stand in the temple.

No matter what life would throw at him, he
chose to be with God. And in entering God's
house, he entered into God's great mercy.

You see, God is magnanimous in mercy. He is
generous in grace. He gives beyond anything you
could ask or expect or hope for.

Even now He invites you into His presence for
worship and praise and fellowship. But you must
make the same decision David made. It can be a
little scary. God is an awesome, fearsome God.
But take the risk anyway.

Let all who run to you for protection always sing joyful songs. Provide shelter for those who truly love you and let them rejoice.

—Psalm 5:11

The psalmist encourages all of us who put our trust in God to rejoice. Not just to make noise. But to recognize God's great work in our lives.

He defends us against our enemies, be they harmful relationships, contentiousness at work, painful memories, tough economic times, or whatever else troubles us.

He will defend us. He will supply us with whatever we need to defeat our foes, strengthen us supernaturally, free us from the fear and doubt that restrict us, protect us from anything that's outside His will for us. And that's cause for rejoicing for those who love His name.

Call on the name of the Lord. Have confidence in the fact that He will defend you. And then you can rejoice in the midst of it all.

DAY 14

Have pity on me and heal my feeble body. My bones tremble with fear, and I am in deep distress. How long will it be?

—*Psalm 6:2–3*

In the depth of despair, David turns to God. In weakness, he begs for pity. In fear, he asks for relief. And he wonders where it is. Why hasn't God answered his pleading prayers?

You've no doubt experienced a dark night of the soul such as David did. Perhaps you can identify with his feelings of abandonment and pain. Maybe you, too, have begged for God's mercy and understanding.

When you reach those depths, take some comfort in the fact that you aren't alone. David has been there. So have all saints who truly yearn to know God and walk with Him. It's part of the process. Accept it as best you can. And keep praying.

Morning will come soon.

My groaning has worn me out. At night my bed and pillow are soaked with tears. Sorrow has made my eyes dim, and my sight has failed because of my enemies.

—Psalm 6:6–7

Pain can be exhausting. Feelings of sorrow, depression, grief, and fear can eat away at us internally to the point that we feel our bodies will waste away.

We lose strength. We forfeit any sense of balance and control over our emotions. We're reduced to groaning, powerless, grief-stricken creatures.

Emotions are very fragile things. When you're working through old hurts or new struggles, your emotions can help you deal with them in a healthy way. Stuffing them, pretending you don't feel grief or fear, won't help at all. In fact, it will hurt you in the long run.

David wasn't ashamed of his grief or his tears. He freely expressed them. But he also turned to his God in trust (v. 9). Remember his example in your times of grief and sadness.

DAY 16

The LORD shall judge the peoples; Judge me, O
LORD, according to my righteousness, And according to my integrity within me.

—Psalm 7:8 NKJV

In an unjust world, it's tempting to call God's
judgment upon people who practice evil. It can
be something as major as a corrupt government
in a foreign country whose track record in
human rights is abysmal. Or it can be something
as minor as a driver cutting in front of you on a
busy interstate, causing you to spill your coffee as
you avoid an accident.

In those cases and everything in between, you
want God's justice on the perpetrators. You ask
God to punish them based on their deeds.

And David does the same. But he also adds today's verse. "Yes, judge them, God," David says.
"But judge me, too."

Would you be so bold as to pray that?

God is a just judge, And God is angry with the
wicked every day.

—Psalm 7:11 NKJV

Why doesn't God do something about evil in
the world? And if God is a good God, why is
there evil in the world at all? And where is He
when the world's evil affects us individually?

The psalmist reminds us that God is just.
Righteousness will prevail. And "God is angry
with the wicked every day." Continually. Until
the end of time.

So why doesn't He do something about it? Ah,
but He will. In His good time. In the meantime,
He offers the same grace and forgiveness to the
wicked that He did to you.

You've already accepted it. Many others will,
too, before the time is up. Perhaps you could foster the same attitudes God demonstrates. Of hat-
ing the sin, but loving the sinner. Of despising
evil, but praying for the evildoers.

Our LORD and Ruler, your name is wonderful everywhere on earth! You let your glory be seen in the heavens above.

—Psalm 8:1

Look up. Lift up your head. Open your eyes and look around you. And praise the Lord.

That can be a tough thing to do at times. When we focus on the frustrations of life, the pain of fractured relationships past and present, the powerlessness we often feel over our circumstances, the last thing we feel like doing is praising the Lord.

But David the psalmist encourages us to let go of all that weight of our existence and look at God. Recognize His power and authority, His magnificence and excellence, His glory and light. He is all and in all and over all—including all those things that tend to keep our eyes off Him.

Pray this verse, and let it usher you into the presence of the living, reigning God.

With praises from children and from tiny infants, you have built a fortress. It makes your enemies silent, and all who turn against you are left speechless.

—Psalm 8:2

Aside from their inherent cuteness, what is it about babies that is so attractive to us? Is it the sparkle in their eyes as they delight in even the most basic elements of life? Is it the tiny sweet sounds they make when content? Is it their absolute freedom to express themselves, even though they are at the same time absolutely dependent on others for basic needs? All of that, and much more.

God has ordained that babies and children express strong praise for Him. You may not have realized that's what they're doing, but they are. And the praise of a tiny baby silences the enemy's tirades against God. And against His children.

Praise God in strength. And He will cause your enemy to be stilled.

DAY 20

I often think of the heavens your hands have made, and of the moon and stars you put in place. Then I ask, "Why do you care about us humans? Why are you concerned for us weaklings?"

—Psalm 8:3–4

You've no doubt done it many times: stared at the stars above you. You know how astonishing the view can be—even though you've seen the same sight for years and years. What do you think about?

The psalmist thought of God and considered the immensity of His creation, all of it the product of God's creative energy.

How little we may feel in comparison to the hugeness of creation. But despite our relative tininess and unimportance, He does know us and care about us and love us. And that's the truly incomprehensible part.

I will praise you, LORD, with all my heart and tell about the wonders you have worked. God Most High, I will rejoice; I will celebrate and sing because of you.

—Psalm 9:1–2

How to have a joyful life: Reflect on the work of the Lord in your life. Remember all the marvelous works He has performed in your midst. Recall how He has rescued you from so many times of fear and frustration. As a result, you'll praise Him.

How is it with you today? Would David's description apply to your life?

You may be burdened by the weight of your problems, particularly if you are actively working through painful hurts. You may focus on what's wrong. And there may be a lot that's wrong. But there's so much that's right. So much that God has done, and is doing, for which you can be thankful.

Enumerate the people, the events, and the blessings that have lifted you up lately. And praise the Lord with all your heart.

DAY 22

The LORD also will be a refuge for the oppressed, A refuge in times of trouble.

—*Psalm 9:9 NKJV*

Refuge. A shelter from danger or trouble. A place to go for safety.

Oppressed. Those who are on the receiving end of unjust and harsh authority. A feeling of being weighed down.

If you ever identify with the latter, you are invited to run to the former anytime you need to. Run to the outstretched arms of the Lord. For He will wrap you up in His love, surround you with His power, and protect you from those who seek to harm you.

Emotional or physical abandonment from a mate, parent, or close friend, deep indecision about what life path on which to venture forth, misunderstandings by coworkers or friends—whatever is weighing you down today, remember a refuge is available.

He is *your* refuge. And He is waiting to welcome you into His protective custody.

The wicked will go down to the world of the dead to be with those nations that forgot about you. The poor and the homeless won't always be forgotten and without hope.

—Psalm 9:17–18

The line is clearly drawn. People without God will perish eternally. If you forget God, He will forget you.

But there's a major exception: people who are in need. God holds in His heart a special place for those who are poor. He will never forget them—though the world tries its hardest to ignore them.

David the psalmist included himself—a king—and his nation, Israel, in the company of the needy because their enemies threatened them with superior military might. They were at risk continually.

So it's not just physical wealth or the lack of it at issue here. It is poverty of spirit, neediness of soul as well. And all those who are experiencing such poverty are comforted with the knowledge that God will not forget them.

DAY 24

Why are you far away, LORD? Why do you hide yourself when I am in trouble?

—*Psalm 10:1*

The times we need God most can sometimes be the very times He seems farthest away. Why?

Why does it so often seem that evil people win when we always lose? Why do they succeed and become wealthy and happy when we struggle to make ends meet and battle with difficulty constantly?

Why must we have to learn the same lessons in life over and over again—lessons about serving, giving, raising children, and all the rest?

Where is God in all of this? He's not far away. He's here. And He trusts you to do what you need to do in all those situations.

It's part of the painful process of living and maturing. Of becoming all that you can be as His child. Of trusting Him, no matter what happens.

Do something, LORD God, and use your powerful arm to help those in need.

—Psalm 10:12

David's words today are the scriptural equivalent of a prayer you've probably prayed often. A prayer that's simple, direct, and heartfelt. A prayer that's immediate and practical. A prayer that can be boiled down to one word: *Help!*

David was surrounded by crafty and smug evildoers who refused to recognize the God of the universe. So he cried out in his own behalf, asking God to remember His children in need and to use His powerful arm in judgment against the evildoers.

Of course, there's a danger: You can become smug in your righteousness.

Even so, remember David's example. When you feel you're at the mercy of some oppressor, call out to God. Ask Him to go to work on your behalf.

Then trust Him to answer in whatever way would glorify Himself the most.

DAY 26

But You have seen, for You observe trouble and grief, To repay it by Your hand. The helpless commits himself to You; You are the helper of the fatherless.

—Psalm 10:14 NKJV

God is the helper of the helpless ones who commit themselves to Him.

Helplessness can be genuine, or it can be imagined. True helplessness can involve economic hardship (as in the fatherless), physical disabilities, or emotional problems. In these cases, God sees the problem and works to solve it. He sees trouble and grief, and He acts to protect those being oppressed.

False helplessness is really laziness, a lack of motivation, a need for true faith. If people are suffering under imagined need or self-pity, He's more likely to let them work through it to better help themselves.

Commit yourself to Him, and He will take care of you. But that doesn't mean He'll do all the work for you. And maybe that's the reminder you needed today.

The LORD is sitting in his sacred temple on his throne in heaven. He knows everything we do because he sees us all.

—Psalm 11:4

You're being watched. But don't let that make you feel uneasy. Rather, bask in its promise of protection, power, and care.

David reminds us that God is ruling over the entire universe. His throne of authority is ever established in heaven. And when our enemies prepare to attack, He sees.

When we're faced with a difficult decision, He sees.

When we're struggling to reconcile with a family member or friend, He sees.

When we're threatened by fear—real or imagined—He sees.

When we battle low self-esteem in our work, or lack of it, He sees.

He sees you inside and out. He knows what you're doing and saying and thinking. He sees; He reigns; He is in control. And you can trust Him totally.

The LORD always does right and wants justice done.
Everyone who does right will see his face.

—*Psalm 11:7*

God delights when He sees those whom He created in His own image display little bits of that image in their lives.

When we're creative, He enjoys the labors of our hands. When we give of ourselves and our possessions, He applauds. When we're merciful, extending grace and forgiveness to those who have hurt us, He cheers. And when we do right, standing up for His will and way, He absolutely loves it.

Of course, we could never display the infinite measure of His creativity, mercy, and righteousness. But He doesn't intend us to.

He beholds us, He watches us, and He encourages us to take little steps as we follow the example of His Son.

And it brings Him great joy. Joy that shines right back on us.

DAY 29

Our LORD, you are true to your promises, and your word is like silver heated seven times in a fiery furnace. You will protect us and always keep us safe from those people.

—Psalm 12:6–7

When you read of God's promises to His children, His power exerted on our behalf, His gracious love abounding ceaselessly for us, you may feel uncomfortably unworthy. But that's the whole problem.

Your doubt about His words for you holds you back from living fully, freely, righteously for Him. If you really took God at His word, wouldn't you be free to live a life of grace and power, reaching out to others in service and support, exercising faith in confronting any threat, standing strong as a whole person embraced by the Father and empowered by His Spirit?

It all starts with believing what God says.

I trust your love, and I feel like celebrating because you rescued me. You have been good to me, LORD, and I will sing about you.

—Psalm 13:5–6

David feels forgotten by God, overwhelmed by his enemies, troubled by problems all around him. And he cries to God, demanding, "How much longer, LORD, will you forget about me?" (v. 1). But through the anguish shines the strength of his faith. And the words above testify to that.

That's trust. No matter what's going on, no matter how distant God may seem, his faith stands. His heart rejoices. He sings in praise. For he acknowledges God's grace toward him in all things—even in the pit of distress.

Could you say the same things David said and mean them?

Why not try, even if the feelings aren't there? Remember what God has done and is doing for you. Praise Him for it. And see if your song doesn't become more genuinely felt as you sing it.

From heaven the LORD looks down to see if anyone is wise enough to search for him. But all of them are corrupt; no one does right.

—Psalm 14:2–3

The human condition is summarized by the psalmist in these poignant, disturbing words. You can imagine the Lord looking down from heaven, shaking His head in sorrow and disappointment, searching for any who might truly seek Him and His will. And He concludes that "no one does right."

All of us pursue our goals, our dreams, our selfish desires. God is secondary—if that.

All this seems a bit harsh. After all, you're trying to seek God. You're following His will as best you can. And that certainly delights Him. But you're also aware of your dark side.

God is still searching. You are still seeking. He has no illusions about who you are—or anyone else on this planet—and neither should you. So don't let it stop you from seeking Him.

LORD, who may abide in Your tabernacle? Who may dwell in Your holy hill? He who walks uprightly, And works righteousness, And speaks the truth in his heart.

—Psalm 15:1–2 NKJV

You're invited to live with the Lord. To make yourself at home with Him. But there's a particular way to get there.

Walk uprightly. Be strong in your faith, confident in His power, moving forward in growth.

Work righteousness. Be active in living out your faith, reaching out to others who need you, being obedient to His will for you as His child.

Speak the truth in your heart. Be aware of what you're thinking and how you're feeling; be transparent with others; be honest in word and deed.

In short, let your life be cleansed and free and full of all good things. Be saturated in His Spirit.

DAY 33

LORD, who may abide in Your tabernacle? Who may dwell in Your holy hill? . . . He who does not backbite with his tongue, Nor does evil to his neighbor, Nor does he take up a reproach against his friend.

—Psalm 15:1, 3 NKJV

Here's another aspect of healthy, godly living: relating to others honestly, good-naturedly, supportively.

First, you should not backbite. No speaking ill of someone else, passing along negative information. Second, you should avoid doing any evil against another. Third, you should not take up a reproach against a friend. No blaming or finding fault.

The flip side is, first, to compliment, affirm, and strengthen others with your encouraging words. Second, to seek to do good, to reach out with support, to offer help or get together for fellowship. And third, to keep clear communication lines open in all your relationships.

DAY 34

O my soul, you have said to the LORD, "You are my Lord, My goodness is nothing apart from You."
—*Psalm 16:2 NKJV*

Without the Lord, what do you have? Without the Lord, where would your soul be?

What kind of life would you be living? How would your relationships be built, and where would they be going? What would you have to look forward to? What would be your goals and priorities?

How different would things be in your life apart from God?

The psalmist asks himself that very question. And he realizes without God, he has nothing good in his life. All would be emptiness, shallowness, and futility.

But with God are goodness, richness, depth, meaning, and joy. With God are all good things.

Think of all the good things in your life. Realize that they are yours in the Lord. And praise Him for them all.

FEBRUARY 3

I praise you, LORD, for being my guide. Even in the darkest night, your teachings fill my mind.

—Psalm 16:7

Life throws us curves all the time. And forks in the road. And roadblocks. In those times, we turn to the Lord for direction. And in His time, in His way, He gives it if we can hear it.

Sometimes we have to wait until the night to hear it. When things seem darkest, coldest, and emptiest, the truth can burst through.

God's guidance shows the way that leads to true life. It is always for our good. And it will always come when we need it most.

Wait for God, even if the night seems dark. He will give you everything you need when you need it. It may not be what you want or expect, but it is the best.

Today, take a few moments to follow the psalmist's lead. Praise God.

DAY 36

You have shown me the path to life, and you make me glad by being near to me. Sitting at your right side, I will always be joyful.

—Psalm 16:11

This verse reveals God's intimate love for you.

It's the prayer of a confident person who trusts God completely. David trusts God to guide him every step of his life. And he knows firsthand the joy and delight of existing in the presence of God Himself.

But maybe it's a prayer that rings hollow for you today. Your path may seem dark and uncertain. The joy and gladness David mentions may be foreign to your experience. Instead, you feel distant from God.

You can be there. You can open your eyes and see the lighted path. Lay down your burden. Give it to God. And ask Him to take you in His arms and make this promise a reality in your life.

DAY 37

You know my heart, and even during the night you have tested me and found me innocent. I have made up my mind never to tell a lie.

—*Psalm 17:3*

God has examined David's heart, even visiting him in the night, probing his actions and motives and thoughts and feelings. And he comes up clean.

Why? Because he has made a life decision. He has purposed "never to tell a lie."

In the Gospels, Jesus noted often that one's words indicate what is in one's heart. A heart that's right with God speaks purity, encouragement, courage, honesty, truth, and love. And it all starts with a decision of the will.

David made that decision. He purposed to speak positively because his heart was in positive relationship with God.

Have you made the decision that David made yet?

DAY 38

Keep me as the apple of Your eye; Hide me under the shadow of Your wings, From the wicked who oppress me, From my deadly enemies who surround me.

—Psalm 17:8–9 NKJV

In the midst of an evil world, surrounded by his oppressive enemies, David asked God to keep him in the center of His watchful and protective care.

The "apple of one's eye" likely refers to the pupil, the center of vision. David asked for God's direct attention, watching David in a treacherous situation straight on. And he asked that God hide him in the protective covering of His strong wings. That image pictures soaring strength and motherly nurturing and protection.

When you face a dangerous situation, or you feel as though enemies lurk around you—whether they're people or memories or personal failures or circumstances—what would you cry out for? Some direct attention. Some strong protection. Some motherly care. That's what David yearned for. And what God offers you as well today.

I am innocent, LORD, and I will see your face! When I awake, all I want is to see you as you are.

—Psalm 17:15

There are times you feel you're asleep. Spiritually, emotionally, perhaps even physically. There are other times you wish you could sleep. But fear and worry and the details of life keep your mind churning fitfully.

In either case, open your eyes. Wake up, and look full into the bright and shining face of your Lord. It's the face of righteousness, truth, and justice. And it's the face of love, grace, and mercy. And it's shining on you to protect you from darkness, to encourage you to take risks of faithful obedience, to satisfy you with wholeness and fulfillment, to remind you of His eternal faithfulness to you.

Look to the Lord for all that you need today. And be fully satisfied with what you see.

I love you, LORD God, and you make me strong. You are my mighty rock, my fortress, my protector, the rock where I am safe, my shield, my powerful weapon, and my place of shelter.

—Psalm 18:1–2

God delivered David from the hand of his enemies. And in praise and thanksgiving, David sang these words to his God.

God is strong. Solid as a rock. Protective as a fortress and a shield. He is your "place of shelter."

His strength is perfect and complete. It's a resource that cannot be exhausted. And it's available to you.

Whenever you feel absolutely weak and defeated, vulnerable to sin or depression or failure, draw on His strength. Run to His fortress. Grab His shield of protection. Hide in the depths of His power.

DAY 41

Death had wrapped its ropes around me, and I was almost swallowed by its flooding waters. . . . I was in terrible trouble when I called out to you, but from your temple you heard me and answered my prayer.

—Psalm 18:4, 6

Have you felt like that? Have you felt as though ropes held you under a torrent of filthy water?

Such feelings cause fear and panic. You yearn to break free and run, sometimes reaching the point of thrashing madly around to escape.

That's the time to call upon the Lord.

He will hear you. He will rescue you. He will break you free from those ropes, gather you up, and take you to a land of clear water and fresh air.

If you feel the need to be cleansed today, cry out to your Lord. You can be assured that He will hear. And He will act on your behalf.

DAY 42

They confronted me in the day of my calamity, But the LORD was my support. He also brought me out into a broad place; He delivered me because He delighted in me.

—Psalm 18:18–19 NKJV

You hear the word *support* a lot today. We all need support. And each of us should be free to ask for and offer support whenever needed.

But as David reminds us, the Lord is our primary support. He holds us up. He keeps us from failing under stress. He gives us courage and power when we allow ourselves to receive them.

David experienced that in "the day of [his] calamity." Surrounded by strong enemies, David leaned on the Lord and found solid support.

What's more, the Lord brought him out into wide open space, free from looming dangers. And He can do the same for you. Why does the Lord do all this? Because He delights in His children.

DAY 43

You alone are God! Only you are a mighty rock. You give me strength and guide me right.

—*Psalm 18:31–32*

Who is God? He is the Lord. He is the Sovereign Ruler of the universe. He is intimately involved in your life. He knows what you're feeling and why. He knows what you need, and He will give it as you can receive it.

He is a rock. Strong, bold, mighty, immovable, unyielding in power. You can stand surefooted on the rock of His truth.

And not only is He infinitely powerful, but He will give you strength. He will endow you with all the power you need if you will only lift your eyes to Him and ask. It may take time. But it will come. And the more you trust Him for it, the sooner it does come.

The Lord your God will guide you right.

The heavens keep telling the wonders of God, and the skies declare what he has done. Each day informs the following day; each night announces to the next.

—Psalm 19:1–2

The universe says volumes about its Creator.

Look up into the night sky, and your heart leaps with awe. Your mind can't comprehend the scope of what you see.

In its beauty and power and complexity, the creation speaks of the God of the universe who created every molecule, who set it into motion, who oversees it every moment even now. The creation never ceases expressing the truth.

And you can hear that truth today. But even more wonderful, you can learn about God directly from Him because you're in relationship with Him. And He knows just as much about your personal universe as He does about the vast natural universe.

In the heavens a tent is set up for the sun. It rises like a bridegroom and gets ready like a hero eager to run a race.

—*Psalm 19:4–5*

Have you watched a sunrise recently? Do you remember the emotions you felt as it shimmered just at the horizon, then burst through, climbing into the sky, waking the world, and shining its burning brightness throughout the land?

Every day the sun rises, like a bridegroom leaving his bedroom full of energy and strength. Like a hero pacing hard and fast to run a race.

David shares a beautiful portrait of the boisterous creative energy that God has set into motion. The sun is only one example of how God has established His universe and keeps it in motion.

The sun speaks of strength, power, consistency, energy, and light. And it's a reminder that all those things and more are available from your creative Lord.

DAY 46

None of us know our faults. Forgive me when I sin without knowing it.

—Psalm 19:12

David has been considering the vast creative work of his God. Surveying the infinite expanse has an interesting effect: He looks inward. And his dark sins come into focus—in stark contrast to the glory and grandeur of creation. And they make no sense to him.

After all, we have a God who seeks to give us all good gifts, who yearns for us to live uprightly and walk with Him closely. And still we seek to live our own way, on our own paths.

David prays a simple prayer: Help me stop covering up the evil I do and say and think because You already know all about it, Lord. Forgive me.

Today, look to the whole of creation that sings about you. Look to its Maker. And be forgiven.

Let my words and my thoughts be pleasing to you,
LORD, because you are my mighty rock and my protector.

—Psalm 19:14

Not only do our big mouths trip us up more
often than we'd like, but our mindtalk can get us
in a lot of trouble, too.

God's Word encourages us to speak words of
encouragement, support, and praise. To build up
rather than tear down. To confront when necessary, but with strength and love balanced. To tell
the truth about a situation, about our feelings,
and about life in general.

So David asks God to help him speak words
that are acceptable to Him. But more than that,
He looks deeper to the thoughts.

Mindtalk can repeat false notions about who
you are and why others act the way they do toward you. Ask God to help you turn your
mindtalk around. It can be a positive force in
your life.

DAY 48

I pray that the LORD will listen when you are in trouble, and that the God of Jacob will keep you safe. May the LORD send help from his temple.

—Psalm 20:1–2

Today, you can draw comfort from the fact that hundreds and hundreds of years ago, David prayed a benediction over you. It was this very prayer.

He prays that the Lord will answer your call for help when you are in trouble—whether physical, emotional, or spiritual. So no matter what strain or struggle you face, call out to Him.

He prays that the God of Jacob will defend you. Just as He delivered Jacob in the Old Testament (Gen. 35). So there's no need to be defensive. He will take care of it.

He prays that God will send you help from His temple. You can draw from the source of all strength and support.

Some people trust the power of chariots or horses, but we trust you, LORD God. Others will stumble and fall, but we will be strong and stand firm.

—*Psalm 20:7–8*

In David's day, Israel was an anomaly. It did fairly well in terms of defending itself, yet it had an unsophisticated army and few weapons of war. The truth is, it had only the Lord God. But that was enough.

As David notes, those who trust in their chariots or horses "stumble and fall." But those who remember the Lord are victorious.

It's easy to trust in chariots or horses. Or today, to trust in jobs, incomes, investments, homes, cars, and other "valuables" of life. Unfortunately, these things usually insulate us from genuine trust in God.

Are you trusting in God? If everything else were removed from your life, would God be enough for you?

Show your strength, LORD, so that we may sing and
praise your power.

—*Psalm 21:13*

The Lord is high above every other living thing,
seen and unseen. His strength is measureless and
unfailing. He never tires. He never needs to rest.

That's the God you know and serve today.
Strong, ready, and able to defend you and uphold
you and pursue you. Above any trouble or pain
you may feel. Yes, His power knows no bounds.

So what do you think about that? How do you
receive that truth today? What will you do with
this kind of strong and mighty God?

The psalmist suggests an answer: Sing and
praise His power. Lift Him up in your praise. Tell
Him how His strength has aided and comforted
you. Sing a song of joy as a child of the powerful
One.

DAY 51

Our ancestors trusted you, and you rescued them. When they cried out for help, you saved them, and you did not let them down when they depended on you.

—Psalm 22:4–5

Trust. Rescue. The two are interrelated, cause and effect.

Trust in God, cry out to Him in distress, and He will rescue you. That was a lesson David the psalmist learned time and time again from the story of the Israelite forebears.

Like Noah, who listened to and obeyed a seemingly odd request of his God to build an ark, but who because of his faithfulness was spared a watery death.

Like Abraham, who obeyed God continually throughout his long life and was rewarded with the heritage of an entire nation.

Like Moses, who despite running from Egyptian authorities for his crimes of passionate justice was used by God to lead a nation to freedom.

The lessons continue if we will recognize them.

You, LORD, brought me safely through birth, and you protected me when I was a baby at my mother's breast. From the day I was born, I have been in your care, and from the time of my birth, you have been my God.

—Psalm 22:9–10

From eternity past, God is. From the beginning of time and creation of the universe, God is. And from the formation of your body in your mother's womb, from your birth into this world, God is.

You may not have realized it, but God has been with you since you were first formed. Perhaps without knowing it, you trusted God even as an infant.

Such things come naturally to the totally dependent. Then, somehow, we lose touch with our connection to the divine. We become more self-sufficient. And who needs God?

But we eventually realize such an attitude doesn't get us very far. And we return to that basic childlike trust in God. And we *know* that He is our God.

The LORD doesn't hate or despise the helpless in all their troubles. When I cried out, he listened and did not turn away.

—Psalm 22:24

Have you ever felt uncomfortable in the presence of an overly needy fellow human?

Now, think about how you approach God with your needs, your failures, your troubles. Do you ever wonder if He feels like avoiding you?

He doesn't. The psalmist assures us of that truth. He doesn't hate hearing about the same troubles. He doesn't turn away when He sees us coming.

No, He hears us. He loves us. He patiently puts up with us. Because He loves us unconditionally, unstintingly, unreservedly.

Don't take His patient forbearance as permission to get stuck in negative mindtalk or trapped by self-pity. He hears, but He'll also do whatever it takes to shake you out of that unhealthy behavior.

DAY 54

You, LORD, are my shepherd. I will never be in need.
—*Psalm 23:1*

It's morning on a hillside. You awake to the breaking day, a cool snap in the air that feels refreshing. The sun beams reassuringly. Its warmth is palpable and growing. All is well. All is right.

You have no need in life. Everything you need is provided for you. Your food is abundant and pleasing. Your protection from wolves and other dangers is assured.

You are content. Satisfied. Fulfilled. For you know that your Shepherd will take care of you.

The Lord is your Shepherd. He loves and cares for you as if you were His child. Because you are.

Spend some moments today on that hillside. Feel what it's like to be shepherded by One who has your every need and desire on His heart.

You let me rest in fields of green grass. You lead me to streams of peaceful water, and you refresh my life. You are true to your name, and you lead me along the right paths.

—Psalm 23:2–3

The Lord your Shepherd invites you to His pasture to feed on satisfying greenery. To drink of the clear, clean water. To follow the path to fulfillment that He sets before you.

Your soul is well fed in the Shepherd's care. Your thirst can be quenched any time you need refreshment. Your soul can be restored whenever you are distressed or needy or empty.

He will carry you, hold you, care for you. He will keep your natural enemies at bay. He will search for you when you have wandered off the right path. And He will not give up until you are in His arms again.

DAY 56

You treat me to a feast, while my enemies watch.
You honor me as your guest, and you fill my cup
until it overflows.

—Psalm 23:5

The Lord invites you to enjoy His hospitality. A
banquet of grace and mercy, of joy and peace.
The feast awaits. The table is prepared.

Even when enemies surround you—frustrations in relationships, difficulties with your
work, past hurts that keep haunting you—you
can fellowship with the Lord. You can let go of
those troubles and feast on His goodness, drawing strength from His presence and His provi-
sions.

The Lord, ever the good host, honors you as a
guest. His favor overwhelms you. He keeps your
cup filled to overflowing. Joy and fellowship
abound.

The invitation stands. Your Host is yearning
to delight in your presence. R.S.V.P.

Lift up your heads, O you gates! And be lifted up, you everlasting doors! And the King of glory shall come in. Who is this King of glory? The LORD strong and mighty, The LORD mighty in battle.

—Psalm 24:7–8 NKJV

The King is coming! And all creation yearns for His arrival to the extent that the city gates come to life expectantly and the doors of the sanctuary are lifted up as though energized. And when they are opened, the King of glory shall come in.

In David's time, this psalm celebrated the king's victory and return to Jerusalem. In the early church, these images were likened to the risen Christ's ascension and return to His heavenly domain.

But His entrance can come even today. Lift up your head, and be lifted up! See who is coming. It is the One who possesses all power and authority. The One who reigns over your life.

The King has come. Let the festivities begin!

I offer you my heart, LORD God, and I trust you. Don't make me ashamed or let enemies defeat me.

—Psalm 25:1–2

When David prayed this prayer, he was under duress, full of distress. And his enemies used that misfortune to taunt and shame him. So he asked God to remove the distress that enabled his enemies to speak ill of him. To remove his feelings of shame at the hands of his enemies.

Shame is a deep, dark wound that scars our hearts. When we feel shame, we are vulnerable to attacks and then to even deeper shame.

But rather than get caught in the downward spiral that shame can cause, we can stop the process by lifting our damaged hearts up to the Lord. We can look to Him for release from the past hurts and relief from the present troubles.

Look to the One you can trust for mercy and acceptance. Drink deep of the healing wine of forgiveness only He can give.

Show me your paths and teach me to follow; guide me by your truth and instruct me. You keep me safe, and I always trust you.

—Psalm 25:4–5

Today, make it a matter of serious prayer to seek God's ongoing direction, moment by moment. Don't wait for the big decisions to seek His insight. Instead, get in the habit of listening to Him continually, of being aware of His still, small voice, of hearing His encouragement along the way.

He will show you the way to walk, the paths to trod. He will lead you in His life-giving truth. He is the God of your salvation. And He deserves constant obedience.

Take your steps, but listen as you do. You'll know if it's the right one to take when you take it.

It's the first step to a life of spiritual vulnerability with the Lord and of healthy dependence on the only One you can really trust.

Please, LORD, remember, you have always been patient and kind. Forget each wrong I did when I was young. Show how truly kind you are and remember me.

—Psalm 25:6–7

Two things David asks God to remember, and one to forget.

"Remember, you have always been patient and kind." It's the way God has related to His people from the beginning. Lord, I count on that acceptance from You; thank You that I can depend on it.

"Forget each wrong I did when I was young." A lot in the past has been forgiven. And if God has forgiven it, it is as though it has been forgotten. Lord, I accept Your total forgiveness of all the sin of my past; thank You that I can depend on it.

"Remember me." In His mercy, God will always keep you in His mind and on His heart. Lord, I acknowledge that I am Yours forever; thank You that I can depend on You.

DAY 61

Vindicate me, O LORD, For I have walked in my integrity. I have also trusted in the LORD; I shall not slip.

—Psalm 26:1 NKJV

To be justified or cleared of some wrong we were alleged to have committed is freeing. To be shown that we were right all along—as rarely as that may seem to happen—makes everything all worthwhile. So the psalmist asks God for vindication from the attacks of his enemies.

But there's an important truth to keep in mind: Vindication can come only if you were right and blameless in the first place.

David the psalmist walked in integrity. His actions lined up with his speech. And that life of integrity is the basis for his request.

Confidence buttresses his prayer: He trusts in the Lord, so he knows he cannot slip.

Next time others have a grievance against you, claiming that you have hurt them, examine your steps. Consider your integrity. Follow David's example.

MARCH 1

Now I stand on solid ground! And when your people meet, I will praise you, LORD.

—*Psalm 26:12*

Sometimes the floor drops out from under you. Or you step into an unexpected pothole. Or you ride an outrageous roller coaster, up and down and up and down.

You yearn for level ground. You hope to see the far horizon and an easy road between it and you. That may not happen. It probably won't happen. But still you can go through life with all its unexpected twists and turns with the attitude of the psalmist—standing on solid ground.

With that kind of level-headed, Spirit-filled viewpoint toward life, you can take on anything. You can handle the potholes and the loop-the-loops, the rocky roads and the deep descents. And when that happens, you can praise the Lord in the presence of fellow believers. You can thank Him for taking you through the pathway of life successfully.

You, LORD, are the light that keeps me safe. I am not afraid of anyone. You protect me, and I have no fears.

—Psalm 27:1

Fear keeps us from risking and reaching out. Fear prevents us from asking forgiveness of those we have hurt. Fear hinders us from asking for the support we need from a friend. Fear keeps us cowering from our tough circumstances instead of standing up in God's power, facing them, and working through them.

Why do we let fear have such power over us? Some of it is automatic, based on old behavior that's hard to unlearn. Part of it is being human.

But as a child of God, you have a source of power and strength you can go to anytime you need to: the Lord Himself.

When you feel fear's cold tentacles encircling your heart, claim God's light and protection. Then take action in His power.

You have helped me. Don't turn from me in anger.
You alone keep me safe. Don't reject or desert me.
Even if my father and mother should desert me, you
will take care of me.

—Psalm 27:9–10

The psalmist acknowledges that God has been his help in times past, then he prays, "Don't reject or desert me." As if God possibly could! Why?

Perhaps because each of us has experienced being left or forsaken by some important people in our lives—friends, relatives, even parents.

Abandonment can be devastating because it programs us not to trust. And that lack of trust blurs over into our relationship with God, who is totally trustworthy.

Even when my mother and my father desert me, David prays, the Lord will take care of me.

There's no doubt of that. God's love is greater than any human's love for us ever could be. Thank Him for that today. And trust Him for it again tomorrow.

I would have lost heart, unless I had believed That I would see the goodness of the LORD In the land of the living.

—Psalm 27:13 NKJV

Losing heart is one of the greatest losses we must deal with because it can devastate our relationships with God and with others. It can keep us stuck in the mud on our growth path. It can cause us to give up healthy steps we're taking. It can make us numb to the Lord who seeks to woo us back on track.

The psalmist, surrounded by evil-speaking enemies, confronted by life-and-death issues, confessed that he very easily could have lost heart.

Unless . . .

David knew that though he dwelt in darkness, surrounded by spiritual death, he would see the goodness of God. He would move into the land of bright sunlight, full of the goodness of God. And that confidence got him through his dark difficulties.

Come save us and bless us. Be our shepherd and always carry us in your arms.

—Psalm 28:9

The psalmist asks four things of God.

"Save us." We need to be saved. In this life we are rushing down a rocky whitewater river headlong toward a churning waterfall that will dash us against terrifying rocks. But God can yank us out of our peril and bring us to dry, solid ground.

"Bless us." We are His inheritance. We belong to Him. We are valuable. We are worth keeping forever. And He desires to lift us up.

"Be our shepherd." God the Shepherd will protect, guide, provide for, delight in, feed, and care for His people.

"Carry us." He will hold us, lift us up, and keep us in His arms—forever.

DAY 67

Honor the wonderful name of the LORD, and worship the LORD most holy and glorious.

—*Psalm 29:2*

Today, recognize that the Lord is glorious. David invites you to praise Him for His utter perfection, His everlasting provision, His enduring love and care.

In our humanity, we cannot approach Him in His absolute righteousness, yet He invites us to come into His presence, to climb onto His lap, to be held in His strong yet gentle arms.

How can this be? How can we accept His invitation? Through Christ.

When Jesus becomes our Savior, our sins are removed and forgotten—past, present, and future. We are wrapped totally in His righteousness and thereby totally accepted by the Father.

Go to the Father in the company of His Son, and worship our glorious Lord.

The voice of the LORD echoes over the oceans. The glorious LORD God thunders above the roar of the raging seas, and his voice is mighty and marvelous.

—Psalm 29:3–4

Listen. Hear the wind growing stronger, moaning with the force of its power.

See it whip the water into frantic white-capped peaks, crashing into each other, endlessly dissolving into still more watery peaks. Hear the water whoosh and spray and splash in the air.

See it move darkened clouds, boiling in their anger, unstoppable in their swift travels. Then hear the thunder roll and crack and blaze in the ears.

Creation can be wild in its power and strength. The psalmist hears the voice of God in the thunder, the Creator speaking through His creation. He is strong, powerful, unyielding in His authority over the waters and the wind and the clouds.

Can you hear Him today? Are you listening for Him?

Your anger lasts a little while, but your kindness lasts for a lifetime. At night we may cry, but when morning comes we will celebrate.

—Psalm 30:5

We know God gets angry over sin and unrighteousness. As a holy God, He cannot ignore it, and He certainly can't condone it.

So when we sin, God may be angry, even though He promises to forgive and forget. And even though all our sins have been cleansed by the blood of Christ.

David reminds us that God's anger is short-lived. He doesn't hold it in and let it boil. He doesn't brood about it until it foments more violently than is reasonable.

No, He becomes angry, and it passes. But His kindness is forever.

In the same way, a time of crying may occur in our lives, but it need stay only a night. We will celebrate in the morning.

That's the flow of life: anger, kindness, crying, celebration. Enjoy the flow.

You have turned my sorrow into joyful dancing. No longer am I sad and wearing sackcloth. I thank you from my heart, and I will never stop singing your praises, my LORD and my God.

—Psalm 30:11–12

Life is full of grief. There are times we must face it and feel it to work through it. But God stands ready to be with us as we do.

The psalmist knew that because he experienced it firsthand. And the result of his trusting in God was surrender and cleansing and dancing.

There is a time to grieve, and then there is a time to put away the sackcloth. To move forward in life and to dance with joy.

You may be avoiding the grief you know you must experience. Take comfort in God's invitation. You may be experiencing grief to some degree, willingly or not. Take hope that it will end in God's time. You may be completing a season of grief. Start dancing and singing and praising the God who brought you through it.

You, LORD God are my mighty rock and my fortress. Lead me and guide me, so that your name will be honored.

—Psalm 31:3

We yearn for God to lead and guide us. We ask for His leadership and guidance daily, usually just tacking the request to the end of our prayers.

God has given us the Bible. And He has given us the Spirit. And that's the way He usually leads and guides us. In fact, as David points out, God in some sense obliged Himself to direct us.

When you face a life decision, or when you want to be aware of God's will for you this day, rely on your Rock. Run to your Fortress. And trust that God will give you everything you need, tell you everything you need to know, one way or the other.

Then will His name be honored through you.

Into Your hand I commit my spirit; You have redeemed me, O LORD God of truth.

—*Psalm 31:5 NKJV*

David the psalmist prayed this prayer of ultimate trust in God. He gave God his very life, his very being, and entrusted it into His absolute care. He kept no strings attached. He made no bargains. He had no ulterior motives. He gave God his spirit and asked Him to exercise authority and care over it.

Why should you follow David's example?

For two main reasons: First, He is the God who redeemed you. He already has claim over your spirit—your life—because He bought it at the cost of His own Son. Second, He is the God of truth. He can be trusted. With every fiber of your being.

A spirit is an impossible thing to grasp on to. But it can be given away. And—paradoxically—only when you give your spirit to God can you truly live a full and fulfilling life.

I pray only to you. Don't disappoint me. Disappoint my cruel enemies until they lie silent in their graves.
—*Psalm 31:17*

David was the king, yet he was surrounded by many who would do anything within their power to overtake him and assume his power. And beyond the treacherous band, he was surrounded by nations that yearned to defeat the little upstart of a country, Israel. Defeat at the hands of either party would be devastating. So David asked the Father to protect him, to prevent his enemies from defeating him.

Though you are not likely in the same situation David was, you may be sensing some disappointment in the form of defeat. Call upon the Lord, and He will rescue you. Teach you. Lift you up. And send you out to battle again. He won't disappoint you.

All who belong to the LORD, show how you love him. The LORD protects the faithful, but he severely punishes everyone who is proud. All who trust the LORD, be cheerful and strong.

—Psalm 31:23–24

Our relationship with the Lord is a deep and unfathomable mystery. Just when we think we understand it, it swallows us up in its abounding grace.

David invites those who belong to the Lord to foster their love for Him. Why? Because He keeps us in His hand. He protects and preserves us from trouble. He fully deserves our loving response to His unmerited favor toward us.

Today, you may not be feeling much love toward God or anyone. Your resources may be dwindling because of the struggles and strains of life and work and relationships and faith.

Take courage. Let go of the bonds of worry and fear that encircle you, and draw strength. You can if you place your trust in God.

Our God, you bless everyone whose sins you forgive and wipe away. You bless them by saying, "You told me your sins, without trying to hide them, and now I forgive you."

—Psalm 32:1–2

Blessed are those whose sins are forgiven and wiped away. The ones who don't try to hide their sins.

If you are a child of God, you're included. You have been pardoned. Freed from the chains of sin that have bound you. Released from the responsibility to pay for it.

In God's eyes, you have done nothing wrong, ever. You have committed no act deserving of any punishment because that punishment has already been meted out in divine justice on the Cross.

Blessed are you! God has poured His favor on you. And you have been freed from anything that could hold you back from being everything He created you to be.

So I confessed my sins and told them all to you. I said, "I'll tell the LORD each one of my sins." Then you forgave me and took away my guilt.

—Psalm 32:5

With God, honesty is without a doubt the best policy. Because He knows everything already.

When you commit a sin—a word spoken with malice, an act of selfishness, a willful disregard of a need you could meet, whatever it may involve—the first thing to do is come to your senses.

Realize what you've done. Accept it. Confront it. Recognize its nature. Then, acknowledge it to the Lord. Don't try to hide it or stuff it or pretend it didn't happen. It's all out in the brightness of heaven's holy light, whether you see it or not.

When you do, the psalmist assures you of God's forgiveness. And the sooner you can recognize that and accept it, the healthier it is for you.

You are my hiding place! You protect me from trouble, and you put songs in my heart because you have saved me.

—Psalm 32:7

At one time or another, all of us reach the point where we just want to crawl into a hole and hide. To shut out the rest of the world from our lives.

We reach our limits with the stresses of life. We become weary over the hassles of dealing with difficult people. We're exhausted by dragging our various burdens around with us, some of which we've carried far too long but can't release.

God understands. His desire is to free us from those stresses, hassles, and burdens. And He's able to do just that.

Today, instead of crawling into a hole, let Him preserve you and surround you with the warmth of His love and the joy of praise. That's not escaping from your problems; it's being delivered from them. Hiding in Him is in reality opening yourself totally to life in all its fullness.

Everyone in this world should worship and honor
the LORD! As soon as he spoke the world was created; at his command, the earth was formed.

—Psalm 33:8–9

The complex, incomprehensible beauty of creation about us sings out in praise to the One
from whose mind it all sprang. Colors, textures,
aromas, sounds—all incredibly rich in their di-
versity and stunning in their magnificence—surround us. And usually, we ignore it all. We take
it for granted. We forget that it had a beginning
and a Beginner.

The psalmist today reminds us to worship and
honor the awesome God who spoke creation into
being.

Recognize the Power behind the world you
live in. Realize He is your loving heavenly Father.
He created you just as surely as He set the universe in order. Thank Him for His creativity, His
power, and His care.

From the place of His dwelling He looks On all the inhabitants of the earth; He fashions their hearts individually; He considers all their works.

—Psalm 33:14–15 NKJV

God has been intimately acquainted with each human soul since the beginning of time. He looks upon the world and sees billions of individuals, one at a time. Each heart, each mind, each soul—He knows them personally. Intimately. Because He fashioned each one individually.

So when your heart is full of joy, bursting with pleasure over an accomplishment or a deepened relationship or a conquered hurt, He feels it, too.

And when your heart hurts because someone has wounded it or you've disappointed yourself by the way you acted, He feels that, too.

Out of the billions of other souls in the world, God sees you. He knows you. He loves you. And He's willing and able to help you.

I will always praise the LORD.
—*Psalm 34:1*

Are your thoughts and words always devoted to thanking and praising and extolling the Lord? Be honest. Probably not. After all, there's a lot going on in your life that you're probably not thankful for. That you'd rather forget about. That you wish, in fact, God would take care of. So how could you be expected to always praise Him?

The truth is, your circumstances may change, becoming worse or better. But God is constant. And He is constantly good and right and worthy of praise.

David is talking about circumstances here. When he wrote this psalm, he pretended to be insane before the Philistine king (1 Sam. 21:10–15).

In any circumstance, God is faithful and powerful and loving. And keeping that truth in mind will keep praises on your lips.

Honor the LORD with me! Celebrate his great name.
—*Psalm 34:3*

Have you given yourself time lately to spend praising your Lord? Exalting Him in your thoughts? Extolling His infinite attributes? Thanking Him for what He's doing, how He's helping you grow, how He's meeting your needs, how He's teaching you?

If you have, you know the blessed sense of joy and freedom such a time can bring.

But David urges us to go one better today: to spend some time with a fellow believer and share the greatness of the Lord.

David invites us to tell each other what God has been up to. Not only do you share steps you've taken toward growth, but you hear how God is working in another's life. And as a result, your joy is multiplied.

DAY 82

If you honor the LORD, his angel will protect you.
—*Psalm 34:7*

The angel of the Lord is God's ambassador from heaven to earth. The messenger who brings God's word and His will to earth. The protector of those who trust in God.

God has sent the angel of the Lord to protect all who honor Him. No enemy can break through; no harm can sneak through. God's angel is on guard. As a result, God's people are delivered from evil and kept from falling.

Nothing can touch you without getting past that angel. And nothing can get past that angel without God's permission.

The Lord is surrounding you even now with protection. So when you face a difficult person, a treacherous place, or a fearful situation, remember that God is with you. And He has sent His angel to protect you.

MARCH 22

Oh, taste and see that the LORD is good; Blessed is the man who trusts in Him!

—*Psalm 34:8 NKJV*

Taste the Lord. It's an unusual invitation.

The Hebrew word for *taste* means "to taste or eat, to discern, perceive, evaluate." The idea is of tasting something to see whether it's good to eat for sustenance and strength.

Now consider the Lord. He invites you to try Him to see whether His presence in your life is indeed good.

David is certain that God is good. If you will only taste, you will see. And seeing, you will trust. And trusting, you will be blessed.

Today, take that risky first step. Trust God for something you've been afraid to ask Him for. Trust Him to enable you to do something you've held back from doing.

Taste life with God, and see how good it is. It's a life of blessed fulfillment.

Do you want to live and enjoy a long life? Then don't say cruel things and don't tell lies. Do good instead of evil and try to live at peace.

—*Psalm 34:12–14*

David offers three practical insights.

First, regarding your tongue: Watch what you say. Strive to build up, encourage, and support rather than tear down, frustrate, or suppress.

Second, regarding your body: Keep away from evil and do good. What you do with your body affects your soul and spirit more than you may realize. If you flirt with danger, sooner or later it will burn you. So seek help, to nurture, to aid.

Third, regarding your spirit: Be a peaceseeker and a peacemaker. Facilitate reconciliation. In your words and your deeds, unite others in the harmony of God's love.

Today, look for ways to put these three practical ideas into action. Then enjoy what happens.

DAY 85

The LORD is there to rescue all who are discouraged
and have given up hope.

—*Psalm 34:18*

Who attached that three-ton weight to your
heart? What elephant is sitting on your chest un-
invited? Who implanted that cannonball where
your stomach used to be?

Actually, when you're discouraged nothing is
very funny. The feelings can be overwhelming. It
seems you're drowning in pain. And no one has a
clue as to what's wrong with you.

Ah, but the Lord does.

The psalmist reveals that the Lord rescues
those "who are discouraged and have given up
hope."

The Lord is near. He is ready to salve your
wounds with warmth and health and life. The
kind that only He can give.

Fight my enemies, LORD! Attack my attackers!
Shield me and help me.

—Psalm 35:1

You have a Champion ready to fight those who
fight against you. He is the Lord God.

You don't have to take care of yourself by yourself. You don't have to fight your battles alone.
You don't have to defend yourself against attacks.

So let it go. And let God do it for you.

Of course, all this depends on whether you are
walking in integrity. And whether God can defend your actions in righteousness.

If He can, when a situation arises in which you
feel you must defend yourself, consciously make
the decision to turn it over to Him.

And sense the stress and fear drain away as He
answers your prayer.

Your mercy, O LORD, is in the heavens; Your faithfulness reaches to the clouds. Your righteousness is like the great mountains; Your judgments are a great deep; O LORD, You preserve man and beast.

—Psalm 36:5–6 NKJV

Sometimes the best thing we can do is to look up, get our eyes off ourselves and our problems, and consider the God who loves us.

Consider His mercy. Think about where you might well be today if not for His gracious provision.

Consider His faithfulness. His care and concern for His children are stubborn and unyielding. No matter what you do or what happens to you, He will be with you forever.

Consider His righteousness. It is immense and infinite, perfect in every way. It is a lamp for your feet, so you may observe where to journey step by step.

Consider His judgments. His will is absolutely right. So you can trust Him wholeheartedly for every aspect of life.

How precious is Your lovingkindness, O God!
Therefore the children of men put their trust under
the shadow of Your wings.

—Psalm 36:7 NKJV

The Hebrew word for *lovingkindness* means "unfailing love, steadfast love, mercy, goodness." The concept is the same as the word *grace* used in the New Testament.

God extends lovingkindness to us, His children. Think about it: It's unfailing, steadfast, merciful, good, gracious love. And it's for you.

David exults in it. He revels in the liberal abundance of it. And he recognizes that as a result of it, people put their trust in God.

Like a mother hen brooding over her chicks, the Father invites you under His wings to be protected, warmed, and filled. There, you can relax and rest. You can be refreshed in the Father's lovingkindness. Today, trust Him for it.

They are abundantly satisfied with the fullness of
Your house, and You give them drink from the river
of Your pleasures. For with You is the fountain of
life; In Your light we see light.

—Psalm 36:8–9 NKJV

Loving God is the highest pleasure a human
being can know. No person, possession, or activity—or any combination of these things—can
come close to bringing the fulfillment and satisfaction that being in the presence of God can
bring.

The psalmist takes us on a mind journey today
through the riches of that holy relationship.

In this relationship are true satisfaction and
pleasure. Satisfaction that abounds from His
presence, pleasure that flows like a clear rushing
river.

In this relationship are true life and light. Life
that bubbles and splashes and refreshes as a fountain, light that warms and illumines all.

Trust the LORD and live right! The land will be yours, and you will be safe. Do what the LORD wants, and he will give you your heart's desire.

—Psalm 37:3–4

Trust the LORD." Let your faith be the rock bottom of your life, solid and supporting, so that you know whatever happens, He is there to turn to.

"Live right!" Not to gain God's acceptance, but to live in the joy of loving God. Be a positive force in the lives of others.

"The land will be yours." It was God's gift to His people. Spiritually, it is yours, too, if you will accept it and live in it.

"You will be safe." Make it part of your conscious being at all times: God is faithful to you and will protect you.

"He will give you your heart's desire." Be aware of all the ways He blesses and provides for you. Recognize how He works in your life, how He ministers through you. And enjoy it.

Be patient and trust the LORD. Don't let it bother you when all goes well for those who do sinful things. Don't be angry or furious. Anger can lead to sin.

—Psalm 37:7–8

In our world, we're surrounded by surreptitious success stories—people who gained wealth and fame underhandedly. Meanwhile, we struggle to make ends meet, never seem to fulfill our simple dreams, and end up frustrated and angry about it all.

The psalmist encourages us to be patient, to trust the Lord to act in justice—because He will. And if we can do that, we won't fret over those who prosper from unrighteousness.

Don't get mad. Don't get even. Don't get fretful. That only hurts you. Leave it in God's hands where it belongs. And start thinking about how you're doing instead of worrying about the wicked in the world. God has it all under control.

If you do what the LORD wants, he will make certain each step you take is sure. The LORD will hold your hand, and if you stumble, you still won't fall.

—Psalm 37:23–24

Just because you're following in the footsteps God has set before you doesn't mean you won't stumble.

David shares that good news/bad news scenario in today's verses.

When you choose to live a healthy life, according to God's Word, responsive to the Spirit, it's good to know that you're heading in the right direction. That you have the blessing of God every step of the way. And yet it's a bit disconcerting to know that you're likely to stumble.

Even so, there's another promise: You won't fall.

Why? Because you're holding the Lord's hand. And He will hold you up.

He will never let go of you. So even when you trip, lose your balance, or start wandering off the trail, He has you in His hand.

Think of the bright future waiting for all the families of honest and innocent and peace-loving people. But not a trace will be left of the wicked or their families.

—Psalm 37:37–38

When you live an honest life—pursuing positive goals, seeking spiritual depth, yearning for personal growth—the end result is peace.

You are at peace with God, with yourself, and with others.

You accept life for what it gives and takes, and learn from it as best you can. You give back to life what you are able to—no more and no less. You stop trying to make things happen as you think they should happen and instead trust the all-knowing, all-powerful hand of God.

Living like that leads to peace and serenity forever and ever.

The alternative—living out of the will of God, in rebellion against His will—has nothing ultimately to offer but death, darkness, and emptiness.

DAY 94

You shot me with your arrows, and you struck me
with your hand.

—Psalm 38:2

You've felt the sharp, biting pain. You've felt the
blow.

Why do you feel so low?

Perhaps it's guilt. But is it genuine or false
guilt? Ask God to show you.

Perhaps it's illness. Ask God for the grace and
strength and healing your body craves.

Perhaps it's a wound inflicted by a loved one,
intentionally or not. Ask God for understanding
about the situation and for the grace to confront
it with loving forgiveness.

Perhaps it's depression over a loss. Ask God for
the ability to grieve and for the comfort only He
can give.

Ask God to help you understand what's going
on and why. If you need to talk to a friend or
counselor to help you get to the heart of the matter, do that today.

Then ask God to bring healing to your body
and soul.

My body hurts all over because of your anger. Even my bones are in pain, and my sins are so heavy that I am crushed. Because of my foolishness, I am covered with sores that stink and spread.

—Psalm 38:4–5

David was physically and emotionally ill when he wrote this psalm. He was suffering deeply in body and spirit, apparently because of a sin he had committed.

He admits he had been foolish. As a result, he had fallen. And the aftershocks of his iniquity reverberated still within his heart.

David was by no means a perfect man. No human is perfect. Yet his heart was tender and open to the Lord's discipline. So he felt the weight of his sins.

Compare his reaction with the reaction of some others today who have been caught in the act but explain it away as nothing serious.

God hears the penitent cries of a wounded heart. And He delights in restoring such a one to strength and wholeness.

Because of my sickness, no friends or neighbors will come near me.

—Psalm 38:11

We stink. Our wounds fester and run. And we may even be contagious.

Often that's how we feel when we're emotionally hurting, dealing with a difficult issue, or working through the process of confessing a sin and making amends to those we've hurt.

Those who love you look at you in those painful times and draw back. Perhaps they are repelled out of a sense of self-righteousness; if so, they probably can't offer you the support you need. Or maybe they don't have the emotional resources to give you what you need because they're dealing with their own issues. Forgive them.

Throw yourself at God's mercy. He promises to be there.

Seek help wherever you think it may be found. And learn to build relationships with those you can trust.

I told myself, "I'll be careful not to sin by what I say, and I'll muzzle my mouth when evil people are near."

—*Psalm 39:1*

We want to be transparent with others who are important to us. We want to be honest and forthcoming with our thoughts and feelings. Yet we also need to protect ourselves from being too open with others who really don't need to know everything about us every time we see them.

David was concerned that he would say something in the presence of his enemies that could be used against him later. So he was constantly on guard, running his thoughts through the sieve of the Spirit of God before speaking them.

And that's a good principle to put into practice today. Get in the habit of thinking through what you're about to say before you say it. And being sensitive to the leading of the Spirit as you do.

I felt a fire burning inside, and the more I thought, the more it burned, until at last I [spoke to the LORD].

—Psalm 39:3

Davidwas about to burst. He was holding his tongue for fear he might say something his enemies could use against him. So he muzzled himself. His emotions churned within him. His mind was caught in a whirlwind of fiery thoughts. Still he held everything in.

Finally, he reached the point where he had to speak. But it wasn't an explosion of emotion, a paroxysm of anger. Instead, he channeled his emotion into a plea to God, a prayer for wisdom, understanding, and forgiveness (vv. 4–13).

God can handle your anger, your fear, your sadness—no matter how deep and broad and wide it is.

So vent it with Him. Let it all out. Be honest with Him. He understands you. He accepts you. He loves you.

Please, LORD, show me my future. Will I soon be gone?

—Psalm 39:4

In the midst of personal turmoil, surrounded by threat, on the precipice of disaster, overwhelmed by emotion, David stopped, took a deep breath, and looked to the Lord. And he asked for perspective.

Lord, let me look at where I am right now. Let me realize how short and fragile my life really is, so I can concentrate on what's important and let go of what is not.

Let me come to terms with the sure fact that this life is transitory; its constant changes ensure that I won't be experiencing tomorrow what I am today. Let me rest in the fact that all those changes are in Your hands, Lord. That You are moving in and through me to bring me closer to You.

Let me understand that without You, I am powerless and frail. With You, I can do all things

[You] pulled me from a lonely pit full of mud and mire. You let me stand on a rock with my feet firm.
—Psalm 40:2

How long have you known the Lord? What was your life like before you were His child? How did you feel? What did you look forward to? What brought you joy? How have those things changed?

Even though you know God now, you may still find yourself in a pit, stuck in the mire. But it's different now. Because no matter where you are, your feet are set firmly on the rock.

God has brought you a long way from where you were. You may feel you still have a long way to go.

Today, don't think about what's left to do. Think about where you've come from and how far you've come.

And join David in thanking God for what He has done.

You, LORD God, have done many wonderful things, and you have planned marvelous things for us. No one is like you! I would never be able to tell all you have done.

—Psalm 40:5

When it seems your friends or family members have forgotten about you, rest assured that God hasn't.

When you become so tied up in self-doubt because you feel no one really takes you or your needs seriously, trust in the fact that God does.

God doesn't give you a call on the phone, stop by for a visit, or invite you to do something fun. God's care for you is on a much higher plane.

He supports you in His arms. He thinks of you and your needs more often than can be numbered. He works behind the scenes to bring you everything you need—perhaps not everything you want, but everything you need. And that's more than enough if you'll let it be.

I have not hidden Your righteousness within my heart; I have declared Your faithfulness and Your salvation; I have not concealed Your lovingkindness and Your truth From the great assembly.

—*Psalm 40:10 NKJV*

Don't keep God a secret.

The psalmist David didn't. He recognized the work God was doing in his life, then revealed its source to others.

God was working righteousness within his heart. Building his character, softening his bitterness, opening his eyes, healing his pain, fulfilling his dreams. David was in the process of growing and maturing, of becoming the person God created him to be. And the credit went to God. David declared God's faithfulness, salvation, lovingkindness, and truth to all around him.

What's God doing in your life today? Tell someone about it! Share it, and spread the blessing of God in your life.

DAY 103

You, LORD God, bless everyone who cares for the poor, and you rescue those people in times of trouble.

—Psalm 41:1

The Bible is filled with admonitions for the people of God to do something about the poor.

The psalmist says to care for them. Realize they are in your midst, even in your neighborhood. And when you think about them, you will surely do something to help—donate food to a food bank, clothing to a shelter, or money to an assistance organization.

But don't just look at "the poor" as meaning people without money. The term includes those who are poor in spirit and health as well. And that opens up a whole new horizon of ministry opportunities.

Open your eyes. Open your heart. And open your resources to those who desperately need them.

As you do, God will bless you and deliver you when you face tough times. That's a promise.

My most trusted friend has turned against me,
though he ate at my table.

—Psalm 41:9

Betrayal. David the king had a close aide and
friend who turned on him. Jesus had a zealous
follower, a passionate friend, who gave Him over
to the authorities—and to death.

Maybe you can identify to some degree with
them. Surely, any betrayal you've experienced
hasn't reached the depth that theirs did. After all,
for them it was a matter of life and death.

Still, it hurts to have a trusted friend turn
against you. If this has happened to you lately,
ask yourself if you know the reason. If you do,
are there amends you can make? And if you
don't, why not ask what the problem is?

Good relationships are hard work. Keeping
them open and honest is a painful process. But
it's well worth the effort.

As a deer gets thirsty for streams of water, I truly am thirsty for you, my God. . . . When will I see your face?

—Psalm 42:1–2

In the depths of your heart, how motivated are you to know God? Is knowing Him and being known by Him your highest priority? Do you hunger for Him in your life, day by day, moment by moment?

The psalmist did. David likened himself to a deer, yearning for cool water to slake her thirst— a thirst that stemmed from the core of her being.

David yearned for God as he did for life itself. He hungered to know Him. So he would make his way to the temple of God as soon and as often as he could.

You can meet God anywhere. Anytime. Under any circumstances. But how much do you want to?

Ask God to add salt to your soul to make you thirstier for Him.

Why am I discouraged? Why am I restless? I trust you! And I will praise you again because you help me.

—Psalm 42:5

In the heart of his being, the psalmist is discouraged and restless. Something is wrong. Perhaps David couldn't even put his finger on it.

You've had days like that. You carry around with you a lethargic feeling of minor depression for no reason in particular. And you can get really frustrated trying to figure out why you feel so down because it doesn't make sense.

The psalmist asks, "Why am I keeping myself down like this? Look at the hope that energizes my life! It's God at work in my life. He offers all the help I need to survive and thrive. And that's worth praising Him for."

Is that a truth you need to remind yourself of today?

O God, our ancestors told us what wonders you worked and we listened carefully.

—Psalm 44:1

When the sons of Korah wrote this psalm, their land was troubled, their nation dishonored. They looked around at what was going on and asked for God's blessing. And what really stung their souls was the realization that it didn't have to be that way and it wasn't always that way.

They remembered the stories that had been passed down from generation to generation. Stories of how God had miraculously blessed, provided for, worked through, and dealt with His people.

Those stories can bring comfort and hope, but they can also shake us out of our complacency and lethargy.

You know the stories. You know how miraculously God can work—not only in the times of the Bible but in your own time. Consider some of your stories that you'd like to pass on. Let those stories work on your heart. Draw hope and encouragement from them.

We are flat on the ground, holding on to the dust.
Do something! Help us! Show how kind you are and
come to our rescue.

—Psalm 44:25–26

You can't get much lower than the psalmists felt.
They were crushed into the dust. Flattened. But
the good thing about being this far down is that
you can only look up. That's what the psalmists
do. In an urgent appeal, they cry to the Lord for
help.

God is a kind, merciful God. He has proven
that time and again, infinitely, gloriously. And
that reputation is on the line.

Keep showing Yourself merciful, the psalmists
cry. Don't stop now!

In the times when you feel you can go no
lower, cry out to God. But first, you must take
your eyes off the dust you find yourself in and
look up to Him.

Are you there today? Trust God to offer His
mercy, rescue you, and refresh you with His presence.

Mighty king, glorious ruler, strap on your sword and ride out in splendor! Win victories for truth and mercy and justice. Do fearsome things with your powerful arm.

—Psalm 45:3–4

Picture the Lord in His glory, the triumphant Groom preparing for His wedding. Realize that you are part of the bride—the church. And He is coming for you.

Joy reigns in the kingdom. The Mighty King—awesome, all-powerful, and victorious—rides in splendor.

He is excited about you. He has won the battle for you. And He is preparing to make you His own.

Knowing Him builds truth, mercy, and justice into your life. Knowing Him infuses you with His strength. Knowing Him ultimately brings joy that knows no bounds.

You have been chosen. You are loved and cherished forever. Rejoice!

I will make your name famous from now on, and you will be praised forever and ever.

—Psalm 45:17

Sometimes you've just got to tell somebody.

The psalmist had been reveling in the glory and majesty of the Lord, and he pledged to tell everybody all about His attributes. And he did.

Thousands of years later, we still read his tribute in Psalm 45. And we join in the praises with him forever and ever.

No one expects you to be responsible for telling all generations about the God you love and serve. But you can tell someone about Him. A neighbor, a coworker, a friend, a relative, a child—somebody. And offer to be a channel through which the Lord can touch that person, too, through a word or a deed you offer in love. That could be the start of a long process of praise that will last for generations.

God is our mighty fortress, always ready to help in times of trouble. And so, we won't be afraid! Let the earth tremble and the mountains tumble into the deepest sea.

—Psalm 46:1–2

The world can be falling down around us, and we need not fear because we know God.

He is a fortress—our protective shelter, haven, sanctuary. We can run to Him at any time, for any reason, and be swept up into His strong arms where nothing can reach us.

He is always ready to help when we're in trouble—He has proven Himself so reliable for generations that there is no reason to fear any situation in the future.

God is present. He is fully with you right now in His entire being. He is locked on to your spirit. And all the resources He offers are available to you.

So when the world is in chaos around you, sense His presence.

Walk through your world fully protected by the peace and power that only He can give.

Nations rage! Kingdoms fall! But at the voice of God the earth itself melts.

—Psalm 46:6

When God speaks, the earth listens. And nothing can stop His will or His word. Not the raging nations or the greatest kingdoms on earth.

God speaks; the earth melts. He doesn't have to raise His voice in any way. He simply utters words. And the impact is unstoppable. Because He is God.

The picture can be terrifying, but it needn't be. You can take comfort from this fact: While the world around you is traveling on an insane path toward self-destruction, God has the power to stop it cold and put it aright.

Why doesn't He do something now about the raging nations of the world? We may never know. Someday He will, and in the meantime, we can only wait and trust.

Look at today's paper. Consider the natural disasters, the political controversies, the degrading trends of society. Let them prompt you to pray about the world. Then listen to what God tells you to do about it today.

Our God says, "Calm down, and learn that I am God! All nations on earth will honor me."

—Psalm 46:10

You can hear God speaking these words to you in the rush of your life: "Calm down. Learn that I am God. I will be honored."

But in this psalm, God isn't necessarily addressing His people. Rather, He is speaking sharply to the godless nations that rage against Him. They war against each other and live in wickedness. They are awash in rebellion against the God of the universe.

And God warns them, as an angry parent would an unruly child: "Realize who you're dealing with because you have no chance of winning over Me."

God puts the little rowdy nations in their place.

So there are two ways of finding comfort in these words: First, take the words for what they say to you in the midst of your life. Second, realize that God is in control over the entire world as well as your little part of it. All is well and will be well.

God rules the nations from his sacred throne. Their leaders come together and are now the people of Abraham's God. All rulers on earth surrender their weapons, and God is greatly praised!

—Psalm 47:8–9

In America, leaders do all they can to appear to be common folk. In England, the royal family—though living in splendor—has its human tendencies in full display, reducing the idea of majesty at times to a bad joke. In other countries around the world, when a leader has been raised to the level of majesty, the reign has often been accompanied by torture, degradation, and depravity.

So what does majesty look like? Look to this passage for a glimpse of the One who is truly majestic, honorable, and exalted. God reigns over all the nations of the world and over every individual life. He rules from His throne in all wisdom and power. And because of who He is, because of His supreme position, He is greatly praised.

Today, turn away from the world; look to the heavens. And praise God.

For this is God, Our God forever and ever; He will be our guide Even to death.

—*Psalm 48:14 NKJV*

Who knows what tomorrow may bring? Who knows how you will die or when?

Will it be sudden, at a younger age than you expected? Will your life be extended, until you're well up in years? Will death be painful? Could it have been avoided?

But what happens after the end? That's where the joy and the mystery are.

Today, you may want to think about some of these serious questions. But as you do, remember that God is your guide right now. And tomorrow. And at the point of death. And beyond, forever and ever.

What's more, He knows what's best for you. He knows the days of your life and has known them from the womb. He knows everything about you. And He loves you enough to be your guide for every step you have left to you.

They trust in their riches and brag about all of their wealth. You cannot buy back your life or pay off God!

—Psalm 49:6–7

We always need more of it; we never have enough of it; we're always losing what we thought we had—if only we had more money.

And yet, the psalmist tells us all the money in the world is useless when it comes to the important things of life.

You can't buy eternal life. You can't even lease it. So if you're trusting in money to get you through this life, you're in for a rude awakening.

If you were dying, you couldn't pay anything to ensure that your soul would enter heaven. Nothing in the world could be given to God as a ransom for your soul.

Which means, in the end, money is worthless.

Only life based on, sourced in, and dependent on God will be accepted in the spiritual bank of heaven.

Don't let it bother you when others get rich and live in luxury. Soon they will die and all of their wealth will be left behind.

—Psalm 49:16–17

It's useless to be envious of others whose wealth has far surpassed yours. It means nothing because when wealthy people die, they carry nothing with them into the next life.

Knowing that fact can create a radical change of perspective in the way you live today. Sure, you may have to do without that luxury sedan or that additional bedroom or any number of things. But you do have eternity. And you can't even begin to imagine how glorious that will be.

Instead of pursuing possessions, pursue peace, justice, and love. Instead of buying things, build relationships. Instead of seeking more money, seek to minister to those around you.

You won't believe the difference that kind of life will make. Not only now, but hereafter.

DAY 118

The Mighty One, God the LORD, Has spoken and
called the earth From the rising of the sun to its
going down.

—Psalm 50:1 NKJV

Sunrise, sunset. The earth has rotated innumer-
able times since the Lord God first spoke it into
being. And every rotation is at His command.
Every inhabitant is under His authority. The
Mighty One, strong and true, has spoken His
will, and day by day He carries it out.

When we consider God on this cosmic scale,
we can easily get swallowed up into insignifi-
cance. After all, there are more than 5.5 billion
souls on this planet. Think of all those life experiences in one day.

But don't get lost in the crowd. You are an individual. And you are always in His sight and on
His heart.

Take comfort in the fact that all is well in the
hands of the Mighty One, from sunrise to sun-
down and all night long. Take what life gives you
today as a gift from Him. Learn from it, appreciate it, honor it, and move on, praising Him as
you go.

Every animal in the forest belongs to me, and so do the cattle on a thousand hills. I know all the birds in the mountains, and every wild creature is in my care.

—Psalm 50:10–11

God is possessive. But He has every right to be: He is the Creator of all. Every living thing belongs to Him. He claims it as His own.

In this psalm of Asaph, God shows us that the sacrifices the Israelites carried out were instituted to point to this truth that everything is God's own. The sacrifices were meant to be not a barren ritual but a meaningful lesson. God didn't need or want ritualistic obedience. He wanted a thankful heart. A humble and obedient spirit. A dedicated life.

Of course, we no longer follow the sacrificial system the Jews did. Jesus Christ provided a once-and-for-all sacrifice on our behalf. But the lesson stands: God owns every living thing. Including you. What He does want you to give is an open, yielded, thankful heart.

Pray to me in time of trouble. I will rescue you, and you will honor me.

—Psalm 50:15

God offers three steps for tough times: Pray to Him, accept His deliverance, and honor Him as a result.

You can count on these three steps. But allow for much anguish, fear, grief, anger, and other tough emotions in the process.

It's just the way we are—weak, untrusting, emotional human beings. It's so hard for us to believe that God will hear our prayers, let alone rescue us from our difficulties.

So time after time, we struggle to rebuild our trust in Him. We do battle with our weak wills and doubting hearts. And time after time, He is faithful to deliver us.

It's the rhythm of life as a child of God. The problems will come. Your faith will be shaken. But in the midst of it all, don't forget that God is ready to hear and answer.

You are kind, God! Please have pity on me. You are always merciful! Please wipe away my sins. Wash me clean from all of my sin and guilt.

—Psalm 51:1–2

David fell prey to lust and temptation. He was, after all, a human being. He looked upon a beautiful woman and wanted her. And took her. One sin led to another until he was mired in a horrible situation (2 Sam. 12).

Nathan the prophet confronted his king. David's heart was still tender and open to the Lord's working. Immediately, he was remorseful and repentant.

David cried out to God for forgiveness. He sought complete cleansing from his sin. He knew in the asking that God would answer.

Still, the prayer had to come first. And in the grip of sin, that can be the most difficult prayer to pray.

Humble yourself. Give God the mud of your life. And receive His cleansing.

I have sinned and done wrong since the day I was born. But you want complete honesty, so teach me true wisdom.

—Psalm 51:5–6

Every member of the human race carries a profoundly dominant gene: sinfulness. Does that mean we should give up to the fact that we're going to make mistakes time and time again?

Of course not. But it does give us understanding of why we do the things we do. And it encourages us to desire complete honesty. We can seek God's truth and wisdom to guide us.

Every action we take, every word we speak, is an outgrowth of the inner life. Obviously, our sinful predilections will color these inner thoughts and motivations. That's why David sought God's cleansing and His guidance where it all begins.

You can follow his example today. Acknowledge your humanity, but ask God for clear truth to empower you to live a more healthy and whole life.

Create pure thoughts in me and make me faithful
again.

—Psalm 51:10

David the psalmist was devastated by his personal failure. His sin overwhelmed him. He
humbly turned to God, confessed his sin,
pleaded for forgiveness, and sought a fresh start.
A clean slate. Pure thoughts. Faithfulness.

God can give the same to you today. You may
be coming through a difficult time personally
that has overwhelmed you with sadness, futility,
or frustration. Whatever it might be, God will
hear the cry of your hurting heart. And He will
honor your desire to be cleansed.

If He could forgive and forget David's sin, if
He could renew a right relationship with David,
He can do it with you—no matter what sinful
blot darkens your heart. And if He can create the
universe, He can re-create pure thoughts and
faithfulness.

They're yours for the asking.

The way to please you is to feel sorrow deep in our hearts. This is the kind of sacrifice you won't refuse.
—*Psalm 51:17*

In a way, the sacrifices pictured what God desired to occur in the heart of the Jewish believer—repentance, worship, thanksgiving, cleansing. They were intended to *reflect* the truth that dwelt within the hearts of His people. Unfortunately, the sacrificial system was reduced to empty ritual—an end in itself rather than the means to the greater end of a rich relationship with God.

In the midst of personal turmoil and remorse over his sin, David the psalmist recognized this truth. The sacrifices God truly desired were not mere actions performed but the emotions and attitudes behind them. David knew that a sin offering was meaningless unless it was given out of a heart full of sorrow.

You can get caught up in ritual just as easily. Search your heart, examine your motives, and come to God. He yearns for you to be honest and intimate with Him.

But I am like an olive tree growing in God's house, and I can count on his love forever and ever.

—*Psalm 52:8*

A tree stands in the courtyard. Immovable. Unshakable. With roots deep in the rich earth, drawing strength, support, and sustenance.

David the psalmist likened himself to an olive tree growing in the courtyard of the temple of God. He had been planted and had grown and was flourishing. He drew health and strength from his surroundings.

An olive tree is evergreen. Always alive, always growing, limbs spreading and greenery flourishing. That was how David pictured himself as a child of God. The question of his place in the world had been settled. He would trust in God's love forever and ever.

How much can you identify with David today? Or are you feeling more like tumbleweed, rootless and moving with the wind?

Trust in God. Settle down with Him. Dig in His soil deeply. And start growing.

DAY 126

From heaven God looks down to see if anyone is wise enough to search for him. But all of them are crooked and corrupt. Not one of them does right.

—*Psalm 53:2–3*

How weary are you of your weak will? How tired are you getting of your seeming inability to do the things you really want to do and the ease with which you fall into unhealthy behaviors? Welcome to the club.

David recognized that to be a human being is to experience failure, selfishness, corruption, and unhealthiness. And there are no exceptions.

But there is an understanding God. He looks and sees reality. It would be nice, perhaps, if He could find someone who really understands Him and seeks Him. But that's just not possible. However, that doesn't stop Him from understanding us, seeking us, and loving us.

You will always experience struggles in this area. Draw comfort from the fact that nobody's perfect. And in so doing, accept God's grace toward you.

Behold, God is my helper; The Lord is with those who uphold my life.

—Psalm 54:4 NKJV

It's comforting to have a friend to turn to when you're troubled and to share your fear, anger, pain, grief, and doubts with. A friend who will listen and try to understand. A friend who will simply be there for you.

David had friends like that. And he acknowledged that those friends upheld his life. They encouraged and lifted him up. And he gained strength through that process.

But David also looked behind the faces of those friends and saw the Lord. In truth, God was his helper—God working through those friends and companions to give him support.

When you've given support to someone, you've sensed the workings of God through you. And in receiving support, you can enjoy supernatural benefits as well.

How sturdy is your support system today? Who would you call if you needed to unload?

Please listen and help me. My thoughts are troubled, and I keep groaning.

—Psalm 55:2

Sometimes you just need to be heard. You need to know that someone hears what's on your mind, what's dragging on your heart.

If you keep your problems and pains to yourself, or if you don't feel heard when you do share them with someone else, your insides build up pressure, like a soft drink bottle that's been vigorously shaken. And if a release does not come, the explosion can be pretty messy.

Don't let it get to that point. Find someone who will listen, even to your complaints. Even to your groaning. And talk to God. God is willing, able, and ready.

God can put up with anything you can dish out. He will listen. He will *hear.* And He will act.

By the way, are you that kind of friend to someone else?

I wish I had wings like a dove, so I could fly away and be at peace. I would go and live in some distant desert.

—Psalm 55:6–7

David the psalmist had reached such a point of frustration and anguish in his life that he yearned to escape.

And who can't identify with that? Sometimes we want to run away from whatever is troubling us—a failure at work, an antagonistic relationship, financial problems, difficult children, whatever it is.

David makes it sound so appealing. The truth is, running away never solved anything. The problems are still there, still weighing on your heart and mind, still unresolved and waiting for your return.

But there is a place you can run and find peace and shelter in the midst of the storm. You can run to the arms of God. You'll find everything you need to face the problems of your life with new strength and courage.

But it was my closest friend, the one I trusted most. We enjoyed being together, and we went with others to your house, our God.

—Psalm 55:13–14

Has a friend ever spoken unkindly to others about you? Has a rumor about you ever crept around, and you discovered someone you thought you trusted had started it? If so, you have a friend in David.

David is shocked to find the source of his painful trouble: his close friend. The times he had shared with him had been enjoyable. Together they had gone to worship their God.

It may be good to remind yourself that though you may have close friends you can rely on when needed, you can't depend totally on any human being. To some extent, a friend will let you down. Some friends may even hurt you deeply.

You can, however, depend on the Lord. In those times you feel hurt and betrayed, don't forget that.

I am attacked from all sides, but you will rescue me unharmed by the battle.

—Psalm 55:18

How does God do it?

Your life is in turmoil, your body is in pain from the emotional hurts you're experiencing, you feel overwhelmed and lost in the battle that is your life, and multiple problems fight against you.

As a result, you're weighed down, turned inward, and left out in the cold. You can't move.

Somehow, in those times, God breaks through. His warm light of love, of acceptance, of reassurance that all is well and will be well, reaches your heart and ignites it, burning away the negative feelings, loosening your faith again, and filling your heart with hope.

Somehow, if you let Him, God rescues you when you get to that low point. He redeems you and renews you. If that's what you need today, ask Him for it.

Our LORD, we belong to you. We tell you what worries us, and you won't let us fall.

—Psalm 55:22

Why do we keep dragging those burdens around behind us? Why do we let them go for a moment, even a day—reveling in the freedom and serenity we experience, the power to look up and reach out—and then return to them and haul them once again upon our weary backs?

The psalmist gives you a promise today: Tell the Lord what worries you, and He will keep you going with new energy and freedom. He will hold you up.

And you can gain hope from the truth that there is a limit to the size of your burden. God will never permit the pains of your life to cause you to fall and not get up again. You can trust Him to honor His promise today.

What is your burden? It's time to throw it into bigger hands.

Even when I am afraid, I keep on trusting you. I praise your promises! I trust you and am not afraid. No one can harm me.

—Psalm 56:3–4

Sometimes there's a known cause for fear. Other times it seems to float through the body and soul without reason.

If you don't deal with it in healthy ways, fear can cause you to get emotionally stuck or angry or depressed. And as time passes and fear grows, you become hardened in your fear.

Shake yourself out of the trap of fear. And consciously put your trust in God. When you acknowledge God's strength and sovereignty in your life, you realize that no human being can have any detrimental impact upon you beyond what you and He are able to bear.

Let go of the fear. Experience the peace only God can give. It is yours for the asking.

You protected me from death and kept me from stumbling, so that I would please you and follow the light that leads to life.

—Psalm 56:13

As we journey through the land of the living, it is difficult to realize that our souls will never taste death. For we are surrounded by death.

Not just physical death through disease and tragedy. But emotional death. The death of relationships. The death of dreams.

The child of God is protected from death. Life may at times feel like death, but it isn't. And you can be assured that your spirit will live forever in the presence of the living God.

God has delivered you from eternal darkness so that you may "follow the light that leads to life." How bright is the path you're walking on? Take a moment today to realize who you are, where you are, and where you are going as God's child. And let the light shine.

My heart is steadfast, O God, my heart is steadfast;
I will sing and give praise. Awake, my glory! Awake,
lute and harp! I will awaken the dawn.

—Psalm 57:7–8 NKJV

A steadfast heart. Confident in the God who sustains and supports. Unshakable in the face of trouble or doubt or fear. Is that your heart today?

If it is, join in singing the praises of the God you trust. Let your heart fly free in worship. Let your glory—your strength, your energy, your self fulfilled—wake up and stretch and roar.

Awaken the dawn with your loud praises, your deep and joyful laughter. Praise the Lord! Sing and be merry!

Drink in God's mercy and peace, and let them pass through to every capillary of your soul and out toward others. Changing them. And thereby changing you.

Everyone will say, "It's true! Good people are rewarded. God does rule the earth with justice."

—*Psalm 58:11*

God will be victorious, and His victory over the evil in this world will cause mouths to drop open and hearts to turn.

His judgment over His enemies will be total. His care for His children will cause the earth to realize that He will reward those who follow Him in love and obedience.

The God you love, the God you commune with daily, is the God who will rule the earth with justice on your behalf and on behalf of all His followers.

Injustice will be forever banished. Pain will evaporate completely. Oppression will be a vague dream. And His reward will be eternal.

You may not sense that victory in your life today. You may wonder where God is and why He withholds His judgment on the evil that surrounds and troubles you. Wait on the Lord. His reward is worth waiting for.

But I will sing about your strength, my God, and I will celebrate because of your love. You are my fortress, my place of protection in times of trouble.

—Psalm 59:16

David's enemies swarmed around him. Their curses and lies bit at him. Their selfish pride irked him. Their bloodthirsty deeds frightened him. Their evil loomed over him. Even so, David sang. His heart kept beating strong for the Lord, for he recognized God's strength and love in his life. He acknowledged that God was his "place of protection" in any time of trouble. And so he sang.

You can sing, too. Whatever your circumstances, whatever your fears, whatever your concerns, you can recognize the power of God at work, a power that's available to give you strength and protection. You can run into His arms and hide. And He will refresh you and send you back renewed in your soul, vigorous in your strength, joyful in your spirit.

DAY 138

You have shown Your people hard things; You have made us drink the wine of confusion.

—*Psalm 60:3 NKJV*

Each of us will pass through times of confusion and weep through the dark night of the soul. That's part of the journey. Ups and downs, ins and outs, it all works together to make us the persons God intends us to be.

In a time of defeat and desperation, David recognized this gritty reality. There are times God must show us hard things.

In those times, we feel confused, unsteady, unsure of our steps because of the truths God reveals about us. We see ourselves as God sees us, and we are overcome by what we see.

Can it be that God still loves us with His whole heart? Can it be that He still extends mercy and grace to us? Yes. And He does so knowing who we really are.

Accept the hard things. Wrestle with the reality of who you are in God's eyes. Know that God loves and accepts you—no matter what.

Help us defeat our enemies! No one else can rescue us. You will give us victory and crush our enemies.
—Psalm 60:11–12

When you face a problem, you can choose from any number of ways to solve it. You can talk to a friend, a pastor, or a counselor. You can let someone else deal with the problem. You can unburden yourself with others, ask for their advice, and receive it. You can even heed it. All of these methods can be good and helpful. God works through other people.

Still, you must remember that in itself, the help of a fellow human being is basically useless. The truth is, another person can't possibly know what to do; the person can't know what's really going on inside you, what's really causing the problem. But God knows all of that. And infinitely more.

And with His help, you can be victorious over problems and enemies.

I feel hopeless, and I cry out to you from a faraway land. Lead me to the mighty rock high above me.

—Psalm 61:2

There's nowhere else to go, nothing else to do. You're up against the wall. Your heart is overwhelmed. And you cry out to God.

You need God to reach down and lift you up onto that rock. It is solid. Safe. It is God Himself.

When you can't go forward anymore, it's time to go up. And you can go up only with God's help.

Cry out to Him; He will hear you. Ask Him to lift you; He will. Seek the stability of the immovable rock of His truth, the unyielding, unchanging reality that can be found only in Him.

From the height, you can see more clearly. You're above the clouds, surveying the problems below. And they look powerless, puny, and not worth being so concerned about.

You are a strong tower, where I am safe from my enemies. Let me live with you forever and find protection under your wings, my God.

—Psalm 61:3–4

During the cold and rainy times of your life, God has shown Himself to be a safe, warm, dry shelter. So you can trust Him now for whatever you need.

In His strong tower, you are removed from the enemy's battle below. You are protected from attack, safe from harm.

In the shelter of His wings, you can be loved, mothered, warmed, filled.

He offers you protection and security, love and care. There have been times in your life when you've accepted His gracious invitation to come into the sanctuary of His shelter, to rest under the strength of His wings, to abide in His presence.

Perhaps today, you—like David the psalmist—will take Him up on His open invitation. Visit. Stay a while. Dwell with Him. Forever.

My soul, wait silently for God alone, For my expectation is from Him. He only is my rock and my salvation; He is my defense; I shall not be moved.

—*Psalm 62:5–6 NKJV*

Wait. Life is full of waiting. As we wait, expectations build. And typically, the expectations become greater than anything reasonable. Which leads not only to frustration in the waiting but to disappointment in the fulfillment.

David reminds his soul to wait in silence and patience for God alone. And to build expectations in Him alone. By doing so, he would never be disappointed.

What are you building your hopes on? A possible meaningful relationship? An acquired treasure? A personal advance in your career? What?

Or are you placing your trust on the rock, the Lord God? He alone can give you what you truly need. He alone is your salvation.

Examine your expectations today. And wait silently for God alone.

Trust God, my friends, and always tell him each one of your concerns. God is our place of safety.

—*Psalm 62:8*

God can handle every tear you could ever shed. He is bigger than any cry you could scream. He is greater than any trouble that may tear at your heart.

Don't hold back. Let it all out. The glorious truth about your relationship with God is that He already knows what you're thinking and feeling and experiencing. You can't surprise Him. He still loves and accepts you.

Being honest with Him enables you to be more honest with yourself. You can feel free to talk to Him about anything at any time.

Trust Him to hear you and answer you. Trust Him not to give you an easy escape from your troubles but to give you a safe place to gain strength and courage to face your concerns. No matter what you're feeling and how deeply you're feeling it, pour out your heart before God.

You are my God. I worship you. In my heart, I long for you, as I would long for a stream in a scorching desert.

—Psalm 63:1

God deserves preeminence in our lives.

He is the source of our strength and wholeness.

He is the beginning and the end of all that we are and ever will be.

He has redeemed us and nurtured us. And He loves us more than an earthly parent ever could a child.

David the psalmist recognized all that. He was determined to seek his God daily. To put aside his cares and concerns and turn to the Lord, the Giver of life.

The yearning David felt for God was deep, just as his body yearned for water in a desert. His relationship with God was a matter of basic necessity.

A soul that thirsts for God will be satisfied, for He is that kind of God. Seek Him out; acknowledge your burning thirst for Him. You will find Him. And your thirst will be satisfied.

Your love means more than life to me, and I praise you. As long as I live, I will pray to you.

—*Psalm 63:3–4*

What would your life be like without God? Think about it. Realize how much strength and comfort you receive from knowing Him. Acknowledge how challenged you are to reach out and care for others because of His love for you. Recognize your hope for continued growth in this life and eternal blessing in the next.

Where would you be without that? What would you do if you did not have God's gracious love to rely on?

David meditated on God's love and realized that it was better than life itself. As a result, he rejoiced in praise, singing and raising his hands in worship and adoration for the One who made life truly worth living.

Praise the Lord with your words and your deeds, and discover true life, abundant life, eternal life.

You bless your chosen ones, and you invite them to live near you in your temple. We will enjoy your house, the sacred temple.

—Psalm 65:4

You have been chosen. Yes, you!

God in ages past chose you and turned your heart toward Him, inviting you to approach Him. That is life's richest blessing, to be chosen to dwell in the courts of God forever. And you are there.

Your surroundings in life may appear relatively drab and uninspiring. But your spirit is there. And by acknowledging that truth, you can experience true satisfaction at the deepest levels of your soul. You can enjoy the goodness of God's dwelling—peace, joy, love abounding.

God's intention in inviting you is not to create pride or self-satisfaction in your heart. Rather, your place in His house can give you the resources you need to reach out and invite others to join you.

Our God, you save us, and your fearsome deeds answer our prayers for justice! You give hope to people everywhere on earth, even those across the sea. . . . You silence the roaring waves and the noisy shouts of the nations.

—Psalm 65:5, 7

How confident are you that God will answer your prayers?

David was profoundly confident. He knew that he knew, down in the depths of his soul, that God would answer His people with "fearsome deeds."

He knew that God was the sure hope of the whole earth and all that lived in it. For He is the Creator of all, and He holds it all in His all-powerful hands.

So when the noise of life reaches an overwhelming volume, you can trust God to still it. Consider the oceans, the constant roar and noise of the waves. He can quiet those waves. In the same way, He can quiet the tumult of the peoples, the roar of pain, the moaning of despair. He can work in awesome power to bring sweet peace, silent solitude, into your heart.

You take care of the earth and send rain to help the soil grow all kinds of crops. Your rivers never run dry, and you prepare the earth to produce much grain. You water all of its fields and level the lumpy ground. You send showers of rain to soften the soil and help the plants sprout.

—Psalm 65:9–10

God's gentle care for His creation is lovingly, tenderly displayed by the psalmist.

The earth yields all that we need because God visits it, waters it, enriches it. His life-giving water suckles all growing things. His hands softly work the earth, preparing it for fruit-bearing. He blesses the growth.

You are clay in His hands. He works in your life as He does the earth. He waters you with the Spirit of joy. He enriches you with every spiritual nourishment you could need. His river washes over you, cleansing you. He provides the grain of life, the necessities of sustenance. He waters your spirit abundantly, showering you with peace, blessing your growth.

Wherever your footsteps touch the earth, a rich harvest is gathered.

—Psalm 65:11

In the land of Israel, the king acknowledged that God was the One who blessed the land and brought forth the abundance of grain and crops and all good things.

The year would be good, David acknowledged, if it was crowned by God with His generous bounty. When the people followed their God wholeheartedly, He set before them a rich harvest.

What He did with the land of Israel and His people under King David, God can do in individual lives. Like yours.

You can acknowledge that God's grace abounds toward you, and that all that you have comes from His hand. You can choose to walk the path of fullness, your hand in His. And when you do, your life is full. You have all you need and more.

How is your year going? How blessed do you feel?

O God, you tested us, just as silver is tested.
—*Psalm 66:10*

Precious metals such as gold and silver are tested for impurities in fire. In the melting flame, impurities bubble to the surface and can be removed.

But the fire is hot. The precious metal must be melted and then remolded into something new. And that's how the spiritual life is at times.

God proves His people in the refiner's fire. The heat of struggle and pain brings flaws to the surface where they can be examined, removed, cleansed. And then we are remade by the skillful hands of a loving Craftsman.

The process is repeated throughout our lives to varying degrees. You may be experiencing the fire of refinement right now.

See it for what it is: an important step in the growth process. You will be made purer and richer as a result of the fire.

Our God, be kind and bless us! Be pleased and smile. Then everyone on earth will learn to follow you, and all nations will see your power to save us.
—Psalm 67:1–2

The psalmist's prayer is full of hope and light. It is worth praying today and every day.

We seek God's mercy and kindness relentlessly because we need them desperately. We yearn for His blessing because we may have missed the blessing we need from others. We seek His smiling face to give us hope and love.

When He answers this prayer, His favor on His children is so obvious that all in our world see a difference. And they are drawn to the light that shines through us from Him.

If you pray that your life may make a difference as a result, God will answer this prayer magnanimously. And His light will shine ever farther.

Our God, from your sacred home you take care of orphans and protect widows. You find families for those who are lonely. You set prisoners free and let them prosper, but all who rebel will live in a scorching desert.

—Psalm 68:5–6

God can care for orphans. Even if your father is still alive, you may feel fatherless. Let God be your Parent.

God can protect widows—those who have lost any important relationship through death or separation. He can help you work through your grief. Let God be your Lover.

God can put the lonely together into new families. If you're on your own, reach out to others. Let God be your closest Friend.

God can bring those imprisoned by poverty or fear or depression into abundance and spiritual prosperity. Let God be your Provider and your Guide.

DAY 153

Blessed be the Lord, Who daily loads us with benefits, The God of our salvation! Selah. Our God is the God of salvation; And to GOD the Lord belong escapes from death.

—Psalm 68:19–20 NKJV

The Lord "daily loads us with benefits." Consider the implications of that statement. Every day, we are literally overwhelmed by an abundance of goodness from the hand of God.

He's a God who not only loads us with benefits but also carries our burdens. At our invitation, He takes the weight of sadness and fear in our lives upon Himself.

Those who know Him are given an escape from eternal death. He is indeed the God of salvation.

What benefits has He loaded on you today? Think them through: the relationships that bring you joy and support and love, the activities that provide an outlet for giving and growth, your eternal relationship with Him. Recognize them. Value them. Praise Him for them.

JUNE 1

Our God, show your strength!

—Psalm 68:28

God has done great and mighty things, awesome in their power. He has done them to you and through you and in you.

He has invited you to push and stretch the limits of your faith, to step forward in personal growth even when you're tired and weary and want to give up.

And He can take what He has already accomplished in your life and strengthen it. Build on it. Improve it. Refine it. Grow it.

You may be feeling rather weak today. There is no strength in your bones or your soul. God can even use that to strengthen you.

If that's where you are, ask Him to strengthen what He has already done for you. He can work miracles with very little to start with.

Just imagine what He can do for you in your strength.

Take courage: You're getting stronger every day, thank God.

I am sinking deep in the mud, and my feet are slipping. I am about to be swept under by a mighty flood. I am worn out from crying, and my throat is dry. I have waited for you till my eyes are blurred.

—*Psalm 69:2–3*

Stuck in the mud, and losing ground fast. David was overwhelmed by distress. He was surrounded by those who sought to harm him. And what was worse, he was suffering the effects of sin he had committed.

David was drowning in his need. He wept to the point of weariness; his throat was dry from screaming for God.

He seemed to be nowhere. Yet, David kept waiting for his God.

His faith may have been tested, but it never faltered. He knew God would be with him in the mud and the flood, in his sadness, fear, and sin. So he waited.

Learn from David's example. Even in his misery, he waited. And trusted.

I am like a stranger to my relatives and like a foreigner to my own family. My love for your house burns in me like a fire, and when others insulted you, they insulted me as well.

—Psalm 69:8–9

Sometimes our personal path takes us far away from home, even from those we love. As we mature as adults, cutting our cords with our parents and family members, finding our own way, making our own decisions, living our own lives, things happen.

Our choices may cause disputes and problems, even estrangement from those who were at one time the most important people in our lives—our parents, our siblings.

In David's case, his spiritual commitments and religious zeal brought separation from his relatives. He was consumed by his relationship with God and the growth it fostered.

Your spiritual or emotional growth may be causing waves in your family. Draw comfort from David's encouragement. Reach out as best you can to your family, but don't stop growing as a child of God.

I am crushed by insults, and I feel sick. I had hoped
for mercy and pity, but there was none.

—Psalm 69:20

We become increasingly overwhelmed by personal problems, loneliness, stress, anger, difficulties, or whatever brings a sense of heaviness and
helplessness to us. We become increasingly needy
for help and comfort. We wear long faces and
sigh pitiful sighs, hoping a friend will pick up the
signs and minister to us, love us, and take care of
us. But no one does.

There will be times you are overwhelmed with
need. And you have every right to get support
and encouragement. But be direct. Ask for it.
Seek out a friend you can trust, and say, "If you
are able to handle it right now, I really need
someone to talk to. And if you can't, that's fine.
Let's be honest with each other."

You'll get what you need. Maybe not the answers you're searching for or the relief from the
problems you yearn for, but you'll get the support that will help you.

I will praise the LORD God with a song and a thankful heart. This will please the LORD better than offering an ox or a full-grown bull.

—Psalm 69:30–31

Some of us get so tied up in the rituals and the rightnesses that we lose sight of what we're really doing. It's right to go to worship services. It's right to read and meditate on God's Word. It's right to pray individually and with others. It's right to be involved in service to those who need it. It was also right to sacrifice oxen and bulls in David's day.

But all those activities in themselves are not what God is looking for in His children's lives. He seeks a heart that yearns to do those things. A spirit that praises Him from the core of its being. A life that lives to know Him and serve Him fundamentally.

The activities spring naturally from a heart, a spirit, a life like that.

Is your heart singing God's praises out of a natural overflow of thanksgiving? Consider your life as a whole: Are you moving steadily toward God? Are you seeking to know Him more intimately?

Let your worshipers celebrate and be glad because of you. They love your saving power, so let them always say, "God is wonderful!"

—*Psalm 70:4*

Worshiping God, seeking Him, arises from a hunger of the soul that cannot be filled until heaven. To the child of God, therefore, all of life on this planet consists of seeking God. And that seeking may express itself in any number of ways.

It can be hard work, and it can come easily. It can be incredibly painful, and it can create the greatest of pleasure. It can be deadly dry and dull, and it can be the most excitement a human heart can bear.

Yet through it all, the psalmist invites worshipers to celebrate and be glad in the process. To have as a foundation for life the sense that after all is said and done, it is well with my soul. My heart is glad. My spirit sings. And as a result, my innermost being says that God is to be honored and praised and adored.

Be my mighty rock, the place where I can always run for protection. Save me by your command! You are my mighty rock and my fortress.

—Psalm 71:3

God Himself has issued a command on your behalf: You shall be saved. The command went forth long ago and is ever in effect, now and always.

The psalmist praised God for this certainty, for he knew God was the foundation of his life—his rock, his fortress. A place of safety he could run to for protection and care.

In our world, we tend to develop few roots. We move frequently, change jobs and even careers often, and find new circles of acquaintances. So in times of fear or loneliness, we may not have developed a place, a safe centering dwelling that is ours, protected from the elements of the world, safe from harm.

God can be that place. Wherever we are, whatever we need, we can run to Him and find ourselves at home. He is our dwelling place forever and ever.

I have relied on you from the day I was born. You brought me safely through birth, and I always praise you.

—Psalm 71:6

When did you first know God? When did you first feel His hand upon your life, His invitation to your soul to be with Him forever? When did you first hear of His love for you through His Son, your Savior? When did you first experience that love in your heart? Perhaps as a child. A young adult. Even later in life.

And yet the psalmist sensed that God's concern for him extended back to the womb. He knew that God had upheld him from birth, had taken him from his mother's womb.

Do you remember your earliest years? What was your understanding of God in those days? Perhaps those days were marked by a childlike faith in the goodness and love of God. You can rekindle those same feelings today. And like the psalmist, praise Him for His long-standing love for you.

I will go in the strength of the Lord GOD; I will
make mention of Your righteousness, of Yours only.
                                    —*Psalm 71:16 NKJV*

I will go in the strength of the Lord GOD."

Every step you take will be in His power.
Every place you travel—from home to work to
the marketplace to a friend's house and back
home—you will be surrounded by His blessing,
His presence, His strength.

"I will make mention of Your righteousness, of
Yours only."

In every conversation, at every opportunity,
tell how God is working, share His grace, re-
count His righteous deeds in your life. Your words
will be seasoned with His grace and charm.

Deeds and words. Actions and conversations.
Every aspect of life upheld and surrounded and
strengthened by God.

That's how you can face life today with fulfillment and satisfaction.

Don't leave me when I am old and my hair turns gray. Let me tell future generations, about your mighty power.

—*Psalm 71:18*

If the standard life span is threescore and ten—seventy years—how much time do you have left? Do you dread thinking of becoming aged and gray? What are your thoughts about that phase of your life? What kind of life do you intend to lead in those days?

The psalmist asked God to remain faithful to him even in those later years. But not for selfish reasons: His goal was to declare the power of God's love to future generations.

What older people do you know today whose faithful example inspires you? How have they ministered to you in the faith?

God has much to teach us through older saints. And He has much to share through us to those who are younger.

He won't forsake you. Don't forsake Him. Make yourself available to His strength, and pass it on.

You made me suffer a lot, but you will bring me back from this deep pit and give me new life. You will make me truly great and take my sorrow away.
—*Psalm 71:20–21*

Life is a series of ups and downs, highs and lows, successes and failures, all to varying degrees. Depending upon where you are on the path of your life today, you may feel a need to praise God in song, cry out in pain, or seek some excitement in the midst of boredom.

The psalmist recognized the ups and downs. When he wrote this, he was surrounded by great and severe troubles. He was in the depths.

Even so, he knew that God would revive his spirit again—as He had in the past, as He would in the future. He would bring him back up from the depths.

Wherever you are, be aware of the cycles. They make life so rich and beautiful. When you're up, don't let the lows surprise or frustrate you. When you're down, find hope in God's constant care for you.

Let the King defend the poor, rescue the homeless,
and crush everyone who hurts them.

—Psalm 72:4

To the poor, the homeless: God is on your side.
He works to bring justice and righteousness to
your world. To provide for your needs. To save
you from harm—physical, emotional, spiritual.
To bring to judgment those who oppress you.

Perhaps you don't feel as though you're part of
that promise. But you can still rejoice in it.

Solomon, son of David, king of Israel, wrote
this psalm as a prayer. His world was infused
with wealth and glory, power and might. He
could easily have been blinded by it all, failing to
see God's will for His creation.

But he knew that the poor and homeless were
always on God's heart. And that influenced his
own way of life early in his reign.

Are you aware of those in need in your midst?
How can you reflect God's concern for them
today?

May the glory of the king shine brightly forever like the sun in the sky. Let him make nations prosper and learn to praise him.

—Psalm 72:17

Relationships form, develop, and sometimes die. Friends and loved ones pass away. Jobs are lost. Possessions are destroyed. Our bodies age and decay. Things change constantly. That's the way life is.

But Solomon reminds us that God endures forever. He is unchanging.

So you can anchor your changing, changeable life to Him and find security and confidence. Think of your life as it has changed in the past year: new environments, new people, new possessions, new expectations, new purposes, new dreams. Can you see God moving through it all? Are you still holding on to Him? Is your relationship with Him growing and changing as well as your life?

God may bring change, but He never changes.

We will always praise your glorious name. Let your glory be seen everywhere on earth. Amen and amen.
—*Psalm 72:18–19*

Life can be full of splendor with God.

When was the last time you watched amazed as the day broke forth around you, the sun beaming through the trees, birds singing, the rumble of the city growing? How often do you marvel at the easy joy a pet exudes? How long has it been since you reveled in the creativity of your fellow humans on display at a gallery or museum? When did you last experience the pleasure of the warm, accepting smile and the long, meaningful hug of a close friend?

Glorious things—the things the Lord God can bring into your life if you will only see them and recognize them for what they are. Keep your spiritual eyes open to the things that God does in the world around you—in His creation, through His creatures, in you.

But I almost stumbled and fell, because it made me jealous to see proud and evil people and to watch them prosper.

—Psalm 73:2–3

A saph the psalmist, a leader of one of King David's priestly choirs, got caught up in the ways of the world, became envious of the powerful and successful around him, jealous of the wealth and success of those who opposed God. His heart became full of anger and bitterness. It cut him off from communion with God and with his brothers and sisters. He almost stumbled until God opened his eyes to the truth. And to the wealth and power that he had unto himself because of God.

What's causing you to slip today? Laziness? Jealousy? Division? Personal rights? Theological wrongs? Sin? The past? The present? The future? It could be any number of things. It's not wrong to think about such things. It is wrong to let those things take your eyes off God so that you're not watching where you're walking.

It was hard for me to understand all this! Then I went to your temple, and there I understood what will happen to my enemies.

—Psalm 73:16–17

What's the use? Why limit yourself because you're a follower of God?

After all, the world around you is buying things, getting ahead, and enjoying it all.

Isn't God supposed to bless righteousness? So why are you having so many painful problems? And meanwhile, the world goes its own blithe way, without God, and seemingly far happier than you. So what's the use?

Those were the thoughts plaguing Asaph the psalmist. He tried to understand it, but it was too hurtful. It didn't make sense. It just wasn't fair.

Then he went into God's house. And looked at life from a new perspective. The end of the wicked is destruction. Eternally.

The way of God's children is joy forever. It's more than fair. It's God's way.

I was stupid and ignorant, and I treated you as a wild animal would. But I never really left you, and you hold my right hand. Your advice has been my guide, and later you will welcome me in glory.

—Psalm 73:22–24

The psalmist confessed that he let his jealousy and anger toward the wicked around him get out of hand. He reached the point of being so foolish that he treated God "as a wild animal would."

But what startled him, and comforted him, was the realization that no matter how outrageous his behavior, God was still with him. God still held him up. He still guided him. He will still receive him into His heavenly glory.

That's not meant to excuse boorish behavior or anger that's out of control. But it can help you come to grips with this fact: If your recent behavior or attitudes trouble you before God, He forgives you. Nothing you can do will ever chase Him away in embarrassment or frustration over you. You will always be held in His hand.

My body and mind may fail, but you are my strength and my choice forever.

—Psalm 73:26

The Bible encourages us to take care of the body—to feed it properly, to keep it in good physical shape, to keep from poisoning it with unhealthy habits.

After all, it is the dwelling place of the Creator of the universe, the true and living God over all.

And yet, we also must come to grips with our mortality. Our physical bodies will die. They will stop working. They will decay. They will return to dust.

What's more, the physical body is the seat of the fleshly nature, the human propensity to sin, to hurt ourselves and others.

Asaph the psalmist makes the point clearly: We can put no trust in ourselves. In one way or another, we will fail. But we have a God who is our strength and our possession forever. A God who willingly shares His strength and grace with His children. Today and forever.

There are no more miracles and no more prophets. Who knows how long it will be like this?

—*Psalm 74:9*

The nation Israel had entered a period of defeat when many were scattered and God's judgment on their disobedience and depravity prevailed.

The psalmist begged God to rescue His people from the taunts of the enemy, to restore their nation's glory, to work again in their midst.

In the meantime, God seemingly couldn't be found. There were no miraculous works; there were no spokespersons for God. No one knew how long the desperate situation would last.

We experience similar periods of dryness and desolation in the spiritual life. And we don't know whether they'll last for an hour, a day, a year, or longer. We can only trust that God knows, hears, and is working through the dryness, using it to teach us, building our trust in Him. The day will come when the floodgates are opened again.

Remember the agreement you made with us. Violent enemies are hiding in every dark corner of the earth. Don't disappoint those in need or make them turn from you, but help the poor and homeless to shout your praises.

—Psalm 74:20–21

God had entered into a covenant agreement with the nation Israel, and in a time of emptiness and desperation, the psalmist called on Him. The people experienced the evil of the world. There seemed to be no hope. Yet God had promised that His people would be His possession forever. What had happened?

The people were suffering from the natural results of years of selfishness and ungodliness. God was using the time to refine them. And the Bible tells us He never really gave up on them. Soon the Messiah would come. Today, God still works in and through His people.

You may be in darkness today, but God's light still shines behind the clouds.

Our God, we thank you for being so near to us!
Everyone celebrates your wonderful deeds.

—Psalm 75:1

Thanks. How many times a day do you say that simple word—to a store clerk, a coworker, a friend? How many times do you mean it? How many times do you say it to God?

In a time of joy, the people of God sang for joy in thanksgiving. Today, let their example guide you to do the same.

What are you thankful to God for today? List as many things as come to your mind. How can you see His hand working through those things? How does His presence come to you through them?

God is the source of every good and perfect gift. Don't get caught taking them for granted. Declare His praise. Thank Him.

His deeds are indeed wondrous, and they prove He is living and active in your midst today.

You hold in your hand a cup filled with wine, strong and foaming. You will pour out some for every sinful person on this earth, and they will have to drink until it is gone.

—Psalm 75:8

Two cups in counterpoint.

One a cup of wine, foamy with spices to enhance its intoxicating effect, poured out and forced upon the wicked of the earth, who must at God's hand drink it to the dregs. It is the cup of judgment. The cup of God's wrath. And the wicked are forced to experience a judgment that staggers their souls.

The second cup holds the shed blood of Christ. God holds it out to those who love Him and follow Him. In Communion we fellowship with Him as we are bought by that blood shed for us. It is the cup of eternal life. The cup of God's unending love. And we gladly drink it with joy in honor of our relationship with Him.

Both cups are offered. All must take one. Which have you chosen?

Our God, you are fearsome, and no one can oppose you when you are angry. From heaven you announced your decisions as judge! And all who live on this earth were terrified and silent when you took over as judge, ready to rescue everyone in need.

—Psalm 76:7–9

The anger of God is an awesome thing to consider. His wrath is to be feared. And one day, all that wrathful anger will be directed toward the wicked of the earth. But not toward you if you're a child of God.

All the righteous anger God has toward sin and evil—even the sin in your life—was dealt with on the cross where Jesus died, taking upon Himself the penalty for that sin. So even though God is fearsome in His power, you have nothing to fear.

Still, God's anger can prompt you to take action, to reach out to one who may be perishing without Him, because such a person cannot stand in the face of God's judgment.

In days filled with trouble, I search for you. And at night I tirelessly lift my hands in prayer, refusing comfort.

—*Psalm 77:2*

Have you ever felt sorry for yourself and liked it? Have you gotten stuck in self-pity, putting up a wall to those who seek to offer comfort, support, and a listening ear?

The psalmist wrote that in a time of trouble, he reached out to God. And yet he refused to be comforted. He kept stretching his empty hand toward the One who could fill it with hope and meaning, but he felt so bad about himself, he couldn't accept God's good gifts to him.

Don't let yourself get stuck. Keep the lines open. Accept what comes. Take it to heart.

You may not get what you need from someone else. But you surely won't if you don't ask for it. And especially if you don't accept what is given. But God is ready and willing to soothe your weary soul and give you the strength you need to take the next step.

When I think of you, I feel restless and weak.
—*Psalm 77:3*

There are times when doing the right things doesn't work.

When you're discouraged and restless, you turn to God and consider His works and His ways. But nothing happens. The troubles still weigh you down.

Or you meditate on His Word, search for encouragement and inspiration, but don't have the strength to overcome the difficulty.

Don't give up. Don't turn your back. Keep on keeping on.

This dry season of discouragement may be something God can use to bring wholeness into your life. There are lessons to learn in the ongoing struggle. You can choose to be open to learn them, or you can ignore them.

Keep open to God's working in your life. Keep meditating on His Word, even when your thoughts echo meaninglessly in your mind. A breakthrough will come in its time.

I call to remembrance my song in the night; I meditate within my heart, And my spirit makes diligent search.

—Psalm 77:6 NKJV

What does your song in the night sound like? It could be a mournful dirge. Or a staccato outburst. Or a stirring song of praise. Or it could just sound like snoring. Sometimes that's the nicest song of the night—it means you're sleeping deeply.

But those nights when you can't sleep, when your mind speeds out of control, rummaging through the problems and trials of your life, you can slow things down with a song or a meditation. Direct your mind toward God. Fashion your helter-skelter thoughts into a prayer. Focus your emotions into a song of the spirit.

Let your spirit search diligently through the corners of your life, seeking to make sense out of what's happening to you. But let your spirit also carry you aloft into the presence of God. And there you can sing.

Then I said, "God Most High, what hurts me most is that you no longer help us with your mighty arm." Our LORD, I will remember the things you have done, your miracles of long ago.

—*Psalm 77:10–11*

Whatever happened to miracles? Why are there no partings of the Red Sea today? Or feedings of thousands of hungry people with a few loaves and fish? Or dead people being raised back to life?

You can read part of the Old and New Testaments and wonder. And then you can realize that there are just as many miracles—if not more—happening right under your nose today: an emotional release; a physical healing; an answer to prayer; clarity in a problem that's confused you for months; a healed relationship you yearned to repair; solid affirmation of a decision you made.

What other miracles in your life can you recall now in God's presence?

DAY 181

You alone work miracles, and you have let nations see your mighty power. With your own arm you rescued your people, the descendants of Jacob and Joseph.

—Psalm 77:14–15

We tend to wonder what God is doing. If we would just open our eyes spiritually and keep them open, we may be witnesses to a lot more miracles in life.

After all, this is the God whose strength is well known in the lives of those who are committed to Him—and the Bible is full of evidence to that fact.

This is the God who has redeemed His people in power and certainty—and many lives can testify to that fact. Including yours.

But it's easy to get so shortsighted and tied up in our own world that we fail to see the wonder and majesty of what God is doing. Not only around us but in us.

So today, stop wondering what God is doing. Start appreciating His miracles in your life. And tell someone else about them.

We will tell them to the next generation. We won't keep secret the glorious deeds and the mighty miracles of the LORD.

—Psalm 78:4

Don't keep God a secret from children.

The psalmist was committed to telling the next generation about the blessings and joys of the Lord. And sharing all about the wonderful deeds He has performed.

We may tend to restrict our children's interaction with God to their Sunday school hour. But the life of the believer is a life of ups and downs, victories and trials, blessings and bitter lessons. And children can understand far more than we may think.

In fact, Jesus often encouraged His followers to act like children when it came to exercising their faith: with innocence, purity, trust, and joy.

God has done amazing things in your life and in the lives of other believers since the dawn of time. Tell your children. Tell other children. You'll experience fresh joy.

God became angry and killed the strongest and best from the families of Israel. But the rest kept on sinning and would not trust God's miracles.

—Psalm 78:31–32

Israel's history can teach us a lot about God. And about human beings.

Imagine experiencing the miracles the Israelites did, and then turning their backs on the One who performed them. Their hard-hearted disobedience year after year brought God's judgment upon them.

His discipline was strong medicine. He was forced to take drastic action. Even so, they continued to sin.

Is your heart tender toward God? Are you still sensitive to His miracles?

Your relationship with God is different from theirs: You're related to Him through Jesus Christ. His anger toward you has already been expressed toward Jesus. Still, it's a good time to ask God to keep your heart open and obedient to Him.

But they tried to flatter God, and they told him lies;
they were unfaithful and broke their promises.

—Psalm 78:36–37

The Israelites at times attempted to act as
though they respected God.

The psalmist noted that they would say the
right words, remarking how wonderful God was,
but they didn't mean a word of it.

They would promise obedience and swear allegiance with one breath, and then go against
their promise in the next.

Speaking words is simply moving your lips,
jaw, and tongue. If the words come from a true
heart, they're worth saying. Otherwise, they're a
waste of breath. The problem with trying to fake
faithfulness with God is that He knows what's
going on in your heart.

Jesus said, "When you make a promise, say
only 'Yes' or 'No' " (Matt. 5:37). Say what you
mean and mean what you say. Especially with
God. Because honesty is always the best policy
with your heavenly Father.

Yet God was kind. He kept forgiving their sins and didn't destroy them. He often became angry, but never lost his temper.

—Psalm 78:38

God's patience is infinite with His creatures. And you can be thankful for that.

Even in the case of the disobedient Israelites, God forgave. He had every right as the Sovereign of the universe to decimate the nation for its incredible faithlessness.

But He was full of compassion. Time after time He turned His anger away; He stilled His wrath.

Humanly speaking, it's impossible to conceive. The people were utterly faithless; God was absolutely faithful. Yes, they suffered judgment. And it was harsh at times. But God's compassion always held it in check; His perfect love reigned.

Today, you may need a reminder that God has forgiven you, that His compassion reaches to you. Accept the love God has for you. Then share it with others.

God remembered that they were made of flesh and were like a wind that blows once and then dies down.

—Psalm 78:39

How could God be so forgiving? How could He justify His compassion for such disobedient people as the Israelites? How could He love a people so totally who refused to love Him back?

Simple: He is God. And He knew they were human beings. They were flesh. Breath. Dust. And because of that, they tended to fall, to forget, to fail.

Yes, there were times of heartfelt love and obedience. Times they worshiped God out of a pure heart. But those times seemed so weak and rare, compared to the many times they spurned His love and neglected His ways.

God could forgive because He was dealing with the people He made and loved. He made and loves you, too. And he accepts you in all your humanity. Don't be so hard on yourself when you fail. Just make sure your heart is in the right place.

Then God led his people out of Egypt and guided them in the desert like a flock of sheep. He led them safely along, and they were not afraid, but their enemies drowned in the sea.

—Psalm 78:52–53

The crossing of the Red Sea. Certainly, it was one of the most thrilling demonstrations of God's love and faithfulness for His people. Love and faithfulness He has toward you as well.

The Israelites had labored for years in Egypt. Under Moses, they gained a precarious freedom and hurriedly took their leave—until it became clear that Pharaoh had no intention of letting the free supply of labor get away.

God's people crossed the waterway on dry land, but the sea swallowed Pharaoh's armies that pursued them. Then God guided His people onward as their Shepherd.

God will move heaven and earth—and sometimes the sea—if necessary to care for His beloved children.

David treated the people fairly and guided them with wisdom.

—Psalm 78:72

As Asaph the psalmist recounted the history of his nation Israel, he came to the pinnacle: the reign of King David.

You've become acquainted with David through many of his psalms. You know him as a sensitive, yet strong, leader whose heart followed hard after God.

Asaph pointed to David as a fair leader who guided his people as God Himself would.

But you also know David as a fallible human who failed miserably at times, who ran away in fear, who suffered serious lapses of judgment, and who bristled angrily at his circumstances.

Just like you. It just shows how powerful God's forgiveness can be. And how it can change your life, too.

Oh, do not remember former iniquities against us!
Let Your tender mercies come speedily to meet us,
For we have been brought very low.

—Psalm 79:8 NKJV

Circumstances have brought you down. Work is torture; important relationships are suffering; financial obligations are overwhelming.

Then you start to think: *God must be punishing me. Certainly, I deserve it for the way I've acted. He's making life hard on me because I've been bad—at least I haven't been the follower I should be.*

That's a common scenario. But it doesn't wash. If you have turned to God in faith through His Son, your past has been taken care of. Permanently. God doesn't remember those "former iniquities." He yearns to send His tender mercies speedily to you if you will receive them.

Accepting His love for you may be the first step to take to climb up out of your low place.

Listen to the prisoners groan! Let your mighty power save all who are sentenced to die.

—Psalm 79:11

The nation of God had lost the very ground on which they lived—the territory given them by God Himself. Their sinful rebellion led to judgment in the form of exile. Foreign powers overcame their land and sent the people away.

Their exile was a spiritual incarceration. It was the lowest point of the nation's history.

So the psalmist turned to God, begging Him to hear the groaning of His people and to preserve those who had accepted their destiny of destruction.

The story of Israel was not over. God showed Himself faithful in later days.

And certainly, He heard their groaning. Surely, He wept over the dreadful disintegration of the nation at the hands of godless enemies.

If you feel low today, know that God hears your groaning; He works on your behalf.

Our God, make us strong again! Smile on us and
save us.

—Psalm 80:3

When the Israelites were banished from their
homeland as judgment for their wicked ways,
they suddenly sobered up.

The psalmist captured their cry to God from a
distant land: Make us—our nation, our honor,
our faith, our lives—strong again.

They yearned for Him to smile on them in
pleasure and delight once again. If only He
would turn His gaze back on them, they would
be saved from their tragic predicament.

Perhaps you're feeling abandoned, too. Unlike
the Israelites, you may be in familiar surroundings, but they may seem hostile, cold, unaccept-
ing. God may feel a million miles away from you.
If so, pray these words. Turn your heart back toward God. And He'll surely bring you home to
Him.

Be happy and shout to God who makes us strong! Shout praises to the God of Jacob. Sing as you play tambourines and the lovely sounding stringed instruments.

—Psalm 81:1–2

The Israelites certainly knew how to party. Throughout the year during certain of the God-ordained feasts, they sang and danced and praised God at the top of their lungs.

Joy reigned. Praise resounded. And the noise was delightful to God. They shouted; they sang; they played all kinds of musical instruments. All for one purpose: to thank God for His provision, His strength, His love.

Unfortunately, many of us today have lost this aspect of worship—free, full, and spirited. Worship that springs from the depths of the soul, releasing the spirit in absolute adoration of the One who deserves it so much.

Today, sing for joy at the top of your voice. Dance. Laugh. Make music. Your heart will overflow with delight. And so will God's.

Listen, my people, while, I, the Lord, correct you!
Israel, if you would only pay attention to me! Don't
worship foreign gods or bow down to gods you
know nothing about.

—Psalm 81:8–9

God is, frankly, jealous. In a land surrounded
by other deities worshiped by other nations, Israel tended to wander off. To give in to the national peer pressure. To worship false foreign
gods.

We wonder how it could happen. After all
they had seen and heard that God had done for
them, how could they turn their backs to Him
and worship carved animals and other fraudulent
representations of power? They could because
they were human. Prone to wander.

Without a commitment of the heart, you will
wander, too. You probably wouldn't worship a
carved idol, but you may build allegiances to relationships or activities or things that are stronger
than your allegiance to God. Hear His admoni-
tion to follow Him more closely. Then recon-
sider the priorities of your life.

I am the LORD your God, Who brought you out of
the land of Egypt; Open your mouth wide, and I
will fill it.

—Psalm 81:10 NKJV

God speaks to His people to remind them of
His commitment to them and His power exer-
cised on their behalf. Despite all that, their love
for Him waxed and waned. Their trust in Him
faltered. Their allegiance shifted back and forth.

That's why reminders are so important. We
tend to need to hear the same things time and
again until they sink deep into the soul. And in
this reminder, God points out that He can fill
every need we may have.

Picture a nest of tiny newborn birds, heads
bobbing and straining, beaks wide open, yearning for that succulent worm about to be dropped
in by the mother bird.

That's how we are with God. We open our
mouths for nourishment, and He provides it.
Physically, emotionally, spiritually.

How expectantly are you waiting to be fed by
God? Is your mouth wide open?

My people, Israel, if only you would listen and do as I say! I, the LORD, would quickly defeat your enemies with my mighty power.

—Psalm 81:13–14

More than anything, the people of Israel wanted to be a nation that stood tall in the world. That was victorious over enemies. That shined as a force to be reckoned with.

King after king struggled to succeed. They tried everything they could think of. And ended up losing the very land they lived on.

There was one thing, however, they neglected to try. Obedience.

God's heart broke over their refusal to listen to His Word, to walk in His ways. If only they would, God says, He would give them what they wanted. Their enemies would be subdued. They would shine brightly in the world.

God calls us to walk with Him, to commune with Him, to dwell with Him. When we do, life's puzzling pieces fall into place.

But I would feed you with the finest bread and with the best honey until you were full.

—Psalm 81:16

Just think what God has given you. Your life contains an abundance of riches that have come directly from His hand. As James puts it in the New Testament, "Every good and perfect gift comes down from the Father who created all the lights in the heavens" (James 1:17).

Consider friendships, a roof over your head, clothing, more possessions than you need, a family, the Bible, a relationship with God Himself, and so much more. Now consider this: God yearns to give you even more if only you would receive it.

He wants you to abide with Him. To face life's troubles beside Him.

Yes, your life contains an abundance of blessings. But are you missing out by letting your relationship with God slide into apathy and casualness?

None of you know or understand a thing. You live in darkness, while the foundations of the earth tremble.

—Psalm 82:5

Look at the people around you today. You will see many who appear to have it all together. Successful, well-dressed, confident. They appear to be going someplace important. They wear pride and self-assurance as badges of accomplishment. But if they aren't children of God, their appearance can be deceiving.

The psalmist captures such people—even leaders of the nations—as ignorant, uninformed, and incapable of understanding what truly is happening around them. They walk about as though in darkness, stumping their spiritual toes, walking without aim or any ultimate direction. To these people, it's as though the earth's foundations are shifting and falling—they stagger around unable to find their way.

So when you see apparently successful, determined people today, realize what might be going on in their souls. And thank God for the stable, secure path on which you're walking.

Our God, don't just sit there, silently doing nothing!
Your hateful enemies are turning against you and re-
belling.

—Psalm 83:1–2

There are times we want God to put our enemies in their place.

God, just haul off and let them have it. They
deserve it. Blast 'em!

After all, they hate You. They rebel against
You.

So, God, why are You so silent? Why don't
You do something about these evil people?

The psalmist begged God to do something
about Israel's raucous enemies.

Sometimes He will, but He usually won't—
yet.

There will come a time when God will judge
the whole world. Those who deserve eternal
punishment will surely get it.

In the meantime, God waits patiently. He
works His will in ways we may never understand.
But we can accept those ways.

DAY 199

Let them be forever ashamed and confused. Let them die in disgrace. Make them realize that you are the LORD Most High, the only ruler of earth!
—Psalm 83:17–18

Let it all out with God. Vent your anger, your frustration, and your hurts. Tell Him exactly what you think. Don't hold anything back.

He can take it. He may or may not answer your prayer in the way you desire. But getting it off your chest will certainly help you feel better, and it will enable you to put the matter into His hands. Just be sure to let it stay in His hands.

The psalmist had every right to complain bitterly about the enemies of Israel. He even had a good motive for wanting God to destroy them: Then the whole world would know that the God of Israel is strong and powerful, greater than any other god or nation.

Sounds good. Sounds honorable. But God tends to do whatever He thinks best. That's why He is God.

Still, He encourages you, like the psalmist, to be as brutally honest with Him as you can be.

LORD God All-Powerful, your temple is so lovely!
Deep in my heart I long for your temple, and with
all that I am I sing joyful songs to you.

—Psalm 84:1–2

The summer has been long and dry; the land
has become parched. Now, with the advent of
autumn, the rains shower the earth. Thirstily, the
land drinks in the water. The mist of the air cools
and soothes. In the same way, your soul thirsts
desperately for communion with the living God.

Can you feel it? Are you aware of your deep
need for fellowship with God? Your heart cries
out for it. Can you hear it?

He is the One who waters your spirit with His
Spirit. The One who nourishes you with light
and life and all things good.

Go to His temple. Spend time in His courts.
Your soul will find what it is so desperate for: acceptance, forgiveness, mercy, love, delight, pleasure, refreshment, renewal. And so much more.

LORD God All-Powerful, my King and my God, sparrows find a home near your altars; swallows build nests there to raise their young.

—Psalm 84:3

In his reverie in the courts of the temple, the psalmist considered the birds that gathered. Some built nests in the porticoes. Truly, they dwelled in the presence of God.

The psalmist yearned to live with God in the same way. Perhaps not physically dwelling within the stone walls, but spiritually—living moment by moment in His presence. And building a nest to find warmth and love in the Lord's house.

God invites you to do just that. To make your mind consistently conscious of His presence in your life. To focus on Him in all His attributes. To experience Him in all His love. To know Him fully as He has revealed Himself.

The birds in the temple court took God up on that invitation. You can, too.

You bless all who depend on you for their strength
and all who deeply desire to visit your temple.
—Psalm 84:5

Blessing, peace, serenity—it is possible to experience these wonderful sensations throughout life.

And here's how: First, find your strength in God, not in yourself. And second, realize you are on a journey to wholeness whose destination you will never reach in this life. But you will surely reach it ultimately.

The righteous believer of Israel had regular occasion to journey on pilgrimage to Jerusalem, capital of the nation and the home of God's temple, His dwelling place. He would set his face toward the city and travel, step by step, over desert and rocky mountain if necessary to make it.

In the same way, life is a pilgrimage. And if you accept the fact that it is a journey of often painful steps toward a glorious destination, you will be blessed indeed.

For a day in your temple is better than a thousand anywhere else. I would rather serve in your house than live in the homes of the wicked.

—Psalm 84:10

Happiness is relative. You may experience a tough time today, and happiness seems only an illusion, a quickly fading dream. But consider the alternative.

The psalmist does. And he comes to realize that a single day in the presence of God, dwelling in Him, communing with His Spirit, is better than a thousand days without Him. Because only with Him are meaning in life, true joy, fulfillment, and rest. In fact, he says he would rather serve in God's house than live with the wicked.

God invites you in. To fellowship with Him. To learn from Him. To delight in His presence.

Spend today in His courts. Meditate on His Word. Speak to Him in conversational prayer throughout the day. Listen for His voice. Accept His love.

And see if you don't agree with the psalmist.

Our LORD and our God, you are like the sun and also like a shield. You treat us with kindness and with honor, never denying any good thing to those who live right.

—Psalm 84:11

God's shining illuminates our path. His powerful shield protects us from spiritual harm. He generously bestows kindness and honor on His children, producing an abundance of joy and peace. In fact, He desires to share all good things.

Ah, but there's a catch: You have to "live right" to experience God this way. That sounds like you have to do something to get God's grace.

Think again. God shares His grace freely with His children. And the only thing you have to do is accept it.

Living right is a *result* of being the recipient of His love and acceptance, not the *cause* of it. So you really can experience God in all His fullness today, no matter how you live.

I will listen to you, LORD God, because you promise peace to those who are faithful and no longer foolish.

—Psalm 85:8

The sons of Korah pray for their nation. And it desperately needs prayer.

After years of captivity, the Lord has allowed the people to return to the land. He has forgiven their sin. He has turned away His anger toward their willful disobedience.

Now what? They stand at the brink of the future. Would God continue to bless and lead? Would the people continue in their newfound obedience?

The sons of Korah wait for God to speak. They want to hear His will. And they know God's message will be one of comfort and hope, of acceptance and promise.

Still, they fear that despite all God's blessings, the people will return to their foolish ways of evil and idolatry.

Today, you stand on the brink of the rest of your life. You may be wondering, "Now what?" Will you turn back to your old ways? Or will you wait and listen for God?

Mercy and truth have met together; Righteousness
and peace have kissed.

—Psalm 85:10 NKJV

The Israelites have returned to their land, and
a new order of life begins.

It is life as it should be lived: a relationship
with God and humanity that continually grows
and reflects itself in everyday life.

"Mercy and truth have met together." God bestows His mercy, and His people live according
to His truth—openly, honestly, transparently,
with one another and with God. His mercy enables us to live true lives; our true lives open the
door for yet more mercy.

"Righteousness and peace have kissed." They
are intimately related and founded upon love.
God's people live righteously, honorably, positively, and God bestows His peace upon them.
His peace encourages us to live righteously, and
our righteous lives bring even more peace.

That's the way it should be. That's the way it
can be.

Justice will march in front, making a path for you to follow.

—Psalm 85:13

This is the way God intends life to be: living a righteous, whole, and positive life—one that's emotionally and spiritually healthy—because you are following in His footsteps on your path.

Thinking about that appeals to your need for hope and encouragement. The problem is, why can't you seem to find those footsteps?

You seek His light to illuminate your path. Sometimes you see it; sometimes you don't. But you keep going. You keep working. You keep taking step after step. And you keep trusting Him in the process.

He precedes you on the path. You can doubt that and look about you in fear and mistrust. Or you can extend your foot and move forward.

That's a risk, but it's well worth taking. Because it's the way life is meant to be.

Make my heart glad! I serve you, and my prayer is sincere. You willingly forgive, and your love is always there for those who pray to you.

—Psalm 86:4–5

David seeks a glad heart from God, a soul that rejoices in Him. So he offers his service to God and makes his request.

And he does so trusting in God's goodness. In His desire to answer the genuine and heartfelt prayers of His people. In His readiness to forgive sins and failures. And in His abounding mercy and grace given freely to His children.

But David's glad heart is not intended to be an end in itself. As he receives God's mercy, he is better able to share it with others. As he experiences God's loving acceptance of him, he is empowered to love and accept those around him.

God's mercy comes in abundance. And that's the way He intends us to relate to others—with an abundance of love and acceptance.

Teach me Your way, O LORD; I will walk in Your truth; Unite my heart to fear Your name.

—*Psalm 86:11 NKJV*

Here is the prayer of a heart that yearns to know God. And that heart senses the distractions that life throws in its way. It is disturbed by the competing demands for its attention from others. And it is torn by its own divisions—inherent desires hindering a pure relationship with God.

Consequently, it's a heart that finds itself in many pieces, each fighting for attention. Like broken glass in the pathway, making the journey treacherous.

That's how David felt. And that's why he asked God to unite his heart into one purpose: to walk in His truth, to fear and honor His name.

Can you identify with his distracted, divided heart? Ask God to pull the pieces back together and bond them with His love. Then your heart will beat with strength and purpose as you walk with Him.

But you, the LORD God, are kind and merciful. You don't easily get angry, and your love can always be trusted.

—Psalm 86:15

Today, take some time to meditate on each word, and record your thoughts.

God is kind. He overflows with love toward you, taking your needs and hurts to heart, working all things together for good on your behalf.

He is merciful, full of mercy and grace toward you, and not because of anything you have done to earn His acceptance.

He is slow to anger. You know how much He must put up with you. His patience is limitless. And if it were not, you would be in big trouble.

He is loving. His love is limitless.

He can be trusted. His way is the only way to true peace and happiness. You rob yourself of richness in life by ignoring the truth of His Word.

He is God. Meditate on Him. Meet with Him. Praise Him.

I am as good as dead and completely helpless. I am no better off than those in the grave, those you have forgotten and no longer help.

—Psalm 88:4–5

The psalmist was so low, he counted himself with those who had already died and been buried. He possessed no strength, purpose, energy, or happiness. Even God didn't seem to remember him any longer. He was totally cut off from God. Isolated. Abandoned. Alone.

Fortunately, the only place to look when you're that far down is up. And though the psalmist felt as though he'd been forgotten by God, he must not have believed it because he was addressing the psalm to God. And he expected God to hear him and answer his prayer.

If you're feeling low, accept it. There may be good reason for it, or you may simply be tired and cranky.

But don't fight it. Instead, talk to God about it. Acknowledge your feelings to Him as honestly as you can. Then let go of them. And move on.

Each day I lift my hands in prayer to you, LORD. Do you work miracles for the dead? Do they stand up and praise you?

—Psalm 88:9–10

In a state of spiritual deadness, the psalmist pleaded for God to hear him. His cries ascended to heaven daily. He reached out for God to the limits of his flesh and bones. And he asked for God to work a miracle. To raise the dead—that is, to give him new life. He considered himself dead, so he must be raised from death. And only God can do that.

Have you reached the point of spiritual death? Your life seems bland, gray, and meaningless. Your prayers bounce off the ceiling. Your emotional pain grips you at the level of individual cells in your body. Your spirit has shriveled up into dust. And they may as well go ahead and bury you.

If you can identify with the psalmist, call out daily to the Lord. Keep reaching out for Him.

Then in His time, watch Him work miracles. Watch Him raise the dead.

Do they know of your miracles or your saving power
in the dark world below where all is forgotten?

—Psalm 88:12

In the dark. That's where the psalmist found
himself. Depressed, afraid, and having no idea
what would happen next. He had forgotten what
it was like to live in the light of God's glory. He
no longer remembered how communion with
God blessed him.

So he prayed. He asked for God to invade the
darkness with His bright miracles. He sought a
new infusion of God's "saving power" into his
cold, dead, dry life.

God delights to answer prayers like that. But
sometimes He waits to answer. And the waiting
can be difficult. But that waiting has a purpose—
to take us to the point of absolute surrender.

You may have longer to wait. Or God may be
ready to flood you with His overflowing grace.
You don't know which will be the case. But you
do know that God will act in your best interests.
In His good time.

Our LORD, let the heavens now praise your miracles,
and let all of your angels praise your faithfulness.
—*Psalm 89:5*

God promises to care for His chosen people
forever. The psalmist recorded His powerful
words of hope and blessing for all generations.
And in response, he burst into praise for the One
who is so worthy.

When God works on behalf of His people, the
world will know it. All creation will acknowledge
it. And will praise His miracles.

And when God works on behalf of His people,
His angels will know it. And will praise His faithfulness.

The truth is, God is working on your behalf.
He has covenanted to be your God forever. He is
providing everything you need right now to live
a whole and fulfilled life.

You may not be hearing much praise for Him
in the world around you. And perhaps not even
in your congregation. But it can start with you
today.

You are the most fearsome of all who live in heaven;
all the others fear and greatly honor you.

—Psalm 89:7

It's not wrong to think of God as a loving Father, a faithful Shepherd, a wooing Lover, a patient Mentor, a concerned Advocate, a gracious Friend, an embracing Mother. We can draw great strength in this cold, prickly world by meditating on Him and reminding ourselves of these characteristics.

But there's a flip side. Ethan the psalmist reminds us that God is "most fearsome." Those of us who live in Him are to honor Him. After all, He is the all-powerful Creator, the righteous Judge, the holy Arbiter. Our fate is totally in His hands—as is the fate of all creation, living and dead.

We get a glimpse of this balance in earthly parents who exercise absolute love and care for their children but know when and how to discipline them. Unfortunately, human parents tend to mess things up sometimes. God never can.

The heavens and the earth belong to you. And so does the world with all its people because you created them.

—Psalm 89:11

True stewardship involves managing every aspect of life, not just money, as a child of God. And it all starts with an understanding that is captured by Ethan the psalmist in today's verse: It all belongs to God. Everything. The heavens and the earth, and even your home and your car. One hundred percent of your income belongs to God.

You own nothing. You may have deeds and receipts, but everything comes from the hand of God. That means you need to care for it, manage it with prudence and wisdom.

God put us on the earth He created for a purpose. Part of that purpose is caring for the earth itself. How are you accomplishing that divine goal?

Your efforts in recycling and managing waste can help. Your work on behalf of the environment can help. It's all part of being a child of God and living on Planet Earth.

But I will always love David and faithfully keep all of my promises to him. I won't break my agreement or go back on my word.

—Psalm 89:33–34

God promises to be faithful to His people because of His covenant with King David. And He promises that that faithfulness will be extended even if David's forebears lived in sin and wickedness. Which is exactly what most of them did.

In the same way, God has covenanted with us. As those who have put their trust in His Son, our Savior, we are His children forever. We can hear Him say these words about us. His love will never be withdrawn. His faithfulness will never fail. His promises will never be broken. His word is good and trustworthy.

No matter what you do or have done or will do, you are secure in Him. Not that your disobedience won't bring about some painful consequences. But even then, you can count on His provision and care.

You have always been God—long before the birth
of the mountains, even before you created the earth
and the world.

—Psalm 90:2

God is always present and always present tense.

He has always been and always will be. The
world we live in may be more ancient even than
our minds can comprehend, but He existed long
before its creation. In fact, He has no beginning.
He is from everlasting to everlasting—without
beginning or end.

God is not time bound as we are. He is above
time, removed from it, yet aware of it. He can
make order out of the past, present, and future
all at once. He can orchestrate future events
while with you in the present.

To our time-oriented minds, we cannot conceive of something without a beginning or an
end. Only God is like that. And God is bigger
than our minds could ever hope to be.

Today, you can draw strength from God's infinity, His timelessness, His eternal presence.

A thousand years mean nothing to you! They are merely a day gone by or a few hours in the night.

—Psalm 90:4

God is timeless. He has no sense of waiting. He's already in the future. And the past. And infinitely in the present.

You look back on yesterday and recall all that happened. In God's sight, the past thousand years are like that single day to you.

The point is, God is still intimately involved in every nanosecond of every moment of every day in every life. Even when the time of your life seems totally out of control, speeding and changing so that you can barely catch your breath, He is behind every tick of the clock. And when life slows down to a crawl through boredom or depression, He still holds you firm in His sight.

Every time you glance at a clock today, remind yourself of God's timeless presence with you. He knows your tomorrows. He'll greet you when you get there.

You know all of our sins, even those we do in secret.
—Psalm 90:8

Moses reminds us that life is short, and there's a very sobering reason for that truth: sin. Sin ages us. Its burden weighs us down. Its power drains our strength. Unless we let God have it.

And He will have it. We may think we can keep certain sins secret from friends or family, but they are clearly revealed in the light of God's countenance.

He knows how you're struggling. He knows the times you give in to sin. He knows every sordid detail that passes through your mind.

But for the believer, all those sins have been dealt with, paid for, removed from the record. That doesn't excuse sin, but it does allow for humanity.

Come clean with God. Open yourself up to His light. Ask a close friend to pray for you and hold you accountable.

God already knows. He certainly cares. Trust Him.

We can expect seventy years, or maybe eighty, if we are healthy but even our best years bring trouble and sorrow. Suddenly our time is up, and we disappear.

—Psalm 90:10

An average life span is seventy years, Moses wrote. But if we manage to live for eighty years, they're only ten more years of troubles and sadness. Not much to look forward to. And then we die anyway. It's over. Life is a brief flicker in the broader scheme of things. And it can be a very painful flicker.

In light of this reality, humanity tries to jump-start itself: "Life is short; play hard"; "Carpe diem"; "Life is tough, and then you die."

There is some good to learn from these marketplace thoughts. In fact, Moses sounds as though he would be in total agreement.

Realize the brevity of life, and take advantage of the time you do have. Take risks. Reach out. Get involved. Get moving. For God's sake. And yours.

Teach us to use wisely all the time we have.
—*Psalm 90:12*

Life is short. It's good to realize that truth and live in light of it.

But when we're young, we think we have all the time in the world. We'll get down to the serious stuff later. And later. And later.

And soon we've found life has slipped away from us. We never got around to doing the things we really wanted to do. The things we felt called to do. The things that could make a difference.

So Moses offers a prayer: Help us, God, to be aware of the brevity and uncertainty of life. Why? That we may know better how to live. With more productivity. More satisfaction. More challenge. More life!

Live in the moment. After all, you only have so many of them left.

And let the beauty of the LORD our God be upon us,
And establish the work of our hands for us; Yes, establish the work of our hands.

—Psalm 90:17 NKJV

The beauty of the Lord—His grace, pleasantness, delight, loveliness—let it be upon us, Moses
prays. Let it envelop us with its breathtaking
power and simplicity. Let it overwhelm us with
its sublimity.

And in so doing, let it establish the work of
our hands. Let it so enrich our lives that everything we do is touched by God's beauty and
grace. Let it soak into our beings so deeply that
the work of our hands takes on eternal signifi-
cance.

Moses has been reminding us that life is short
and time is precious. But any activity we would
pursue to fill and use that time without God is
useless.

That's why he writes this summary challenge,
this potent prayer. Without God's gracious direction, without His empowerment, the work of
our hands is fruitless.

He will spread his wings over you and keep you secure. His faithfulness is like a shield or a city wall.

—Psalm 91:4

A mother bird is a fascinating creature, capable of warm, careful concern, on the one hand, and fierce protective defense of her children, on the other.

And in that illustration you can catch a glimpse of God's care for you. God covers you with His wings so you are warm and protected from the elements. You are able to grow as you should. All your needs are provided. And you can nest in His love.

And when you do venture out from the nest, trying your own wings, you can always fly back to Him and find refuge and safety under His wings.

As you grow, He provides the defense and strength you need as you face the world. Wherever you go, you can take His truth with you as a shield from enemy attack and from emotional harm.

Today, nest with Him for a while. Let Him equip you to take flight.

You shall not be afraid of the terror by night, Nor of the arrow that flies by day, Nor of the pestilence that walks in darkness, Nor of the destruction that lays waste at noonday.

—Psalm 91:5–6 NKJV

The psalmist makes real the fears of life by considering them as living beings that fly and walk and leave a wake of destruction in their path. In fact, in the ancient world each evil was considered a god or a demon.

We may scoff at such notions in our sophisticated culture. But we still feel the fears. The deep, stabbing fear of terror by night—fear of the unknown or of the unexpected. The sharp pain of the fear of harm—physical or emotional. The dread that overcomes us through the fear of sickness. The panic of victimization at the hands of a world gone mad with ungodliness.

But the psalmist offers hope. With God, "you shall not be afraid." It's a promise. And it's based on God's character of protecting and providing for His children.

God will command his angels to protect you wherever you go. They will carry you in their arms, and
you won't hurt your feet on the stones.

—Psalm 91:11–12

Angels are beings created by God to perform His will throughout the universe. They are His powerful messengers, glorious to behold. Full of light and majesty, yet always pointing the way to their Master.

Do you believe that? Do you consciously wonder what God's angels are doing on your behalf at this very moment?

Apparently, they are hard at work for you. God sends them to minister to you behind the scenes. Protecting you, holding you up, keeping you even from stubbing your toe sometimes.

Of course, angels have limits. And you have a sinful will.

Still, it's good to keep in mind that they have been sent by God to you. And that's just one more way God shows His abundant love and care for you.

Because he has set his love upon Me, therefore I will
deliver him; I will set him on high, because he has
known My name.

—*Psalm 91:14 NKJV*

In response to the prayer of the psalmist, God
answers. And His words can bring you hope and
challenge in your walk.

Notice the cause-and-effect relationship.
Cause: The believer "has set his love upon Me."
Effect: "I will deliver him." Cause: The believer
"has known My name." Effect: "I will set him on
high."

The truth is, your relationship with God is
certain, no matter what you do. However, the
more you put into it, the more you'll get out of
it.

Putting more into it involves knowing God as
He is. Knowing Him as a living being. Walking
with Him. Placing your love and trust in Him.
Yearning for more of Him. Pursuing Him and
His will for you daily.

Everything you do makes me happy, and I sing joyful songs.

—Psalm 92:4

Consider God's work around you: His awesome, infinite creation, its beauty and order, its color and variety, its immensity and detail.

Consider how He meets your needs for life and health and inspiration and fulfillment through His creation: witnessing a breathtaking sunset, waking to the cheery chaos of the songs of many birds, walking through an autumn-painted forest, gaining strength through the rhythm of the ocean waves.

Consider, too, the work He has done in your life: learning how to deal with character flaws or deep-seated needs, enjoying the friendships He has brought into your life, struggling successfully through a difficult relationship. Throughout the day, consider God's work around you and in you, and like the psalmist, "sing joyful songs."

They will take root in your house, LORD God, and
they will do well. They will be like trees that stay
healthy and fruitful, even when they are old.

—Psalm 92:13–14

Think of the people you know in your church
or neighborhood who almost visibly shine with
God's love and wisdom. Typically, they're older
folks, having walked with God for many years,
struggling, learning, coping, growing.

They shine because they have flourished in the
presence of God. Even when they are older, the
psalmist points out, they still bear fruit. And they
can't help having a positive impact on others'
lives.

How do you see yourself in later years? Is this
the picture that you'd like to be used to describe
you?

Then now is the time to "take root" in the
house of the Lord. That means living a life committed to growing with God. Build a life like that
now, and you'll enjoy healthy and fruitful years as
long as you walk this earth.

Our LORD, you are King! Majesty and power are your royal robes. You put the world in place, and it will never be moved.

—Psalm 93:1

Whatever is capturing your attention other than God, just for today, give it a rest. And turn your eyes to the Lord.

Meditate on His majesty. He reigns over all creation—the immense whole of it and every single part of it. He is a God of grandeur and kingly authority. And He can rule in your life.

Meditate on His strength. He is surrounded by power—His all-consuming power. He is able to do anything His will declares.

And because of who He is, the world—even your world—is put in place. It is in His gaze, under His authority, and in His hands. It cannot be moved or thrown out of balance.

Soak in these truths. Then look again at your problems. Watch what happens to them. And to you.

God gave us ears and eyes! Can't he hear and see?
—*Psalm 94:9*

God just doesn't hear my cries. He must not see the mess I'm in. Otherwise He would have done something for me by now!

Have you ever had thoughts like these? If so, the psalmist throws them right back at you.

And his argument is forceful: How can the One who created ears not hear? And how can the One who gave us eyes not see?

Yes, God hears. Surely, He sees. But most important, He knows best.

It may seem that He is slow to respond to your pleas. Deaf to your cries. Blind to your needs. But the truth is, He is working out His perfect plan for you. He is bringing to you everything you need to survive and even flourish today.

So put your trust in the One who hears all, sees all, knows all, and loves all. Especially you.

God instructs the nations and gives knowledge to us all. Won't he also correct us?

—Psalm 94:10

The world is one immense classroom. Life is one major advanced course. And God Himself is the Teacher.

He instructs the nations. He corrects and disciplines when necessary. He shares the knowledge of the ages, insight into the present, and hope for the future.

Some of us in the class tend to let our thoughts wander. Or fall asleep. Or worse, play hooky. Some of us don't even realize we're taking a course.

But there are a few who struggle to hear the Teacher speak, meditate on the truth they hear, and work hard to put the lessons learned into practice.

What kind of student are you? Think today of God as your Teacher. One who yearns to see you grow and develop in wisdom and knowledge and character. One who works hard at leading you along the most effective path of progress.

The LORD knows how useless our plans really are.
—*Psalm 94:11*

There are times when we think we have it all figured out.

We make our plans and assume they will happen. We decide we know why we behave habitually in a certain harmful way. We recognize others' problems and try to help them understand, too. We think we understand God.

Certainly, God gave us minds to use. To ponder, to question, even to doubt. To work through our thoughts and feelings. To be stimulated and expanded intellectually. To enjoy thoughtful conversation, reading, and writing.

But we should engage in all that with one truth firmly in mind: *Our* thoughts are futile. With the limits of our comprehension and intelligence, we really understand nothing.

God knows all our thoughts. Certainly, He must chuckle at times—perhaps even laugh uproariously. Because He knows the truth—all truth. He *is* truth.

If you had not helped me, LORD, I would soon have gone to the land of silence. . . . And when I was burdened with worries, you comforted me and made me feel secure.

—Psalm 94:17, 19

Have you ever felt you'd die if you didn't get some relief? You're dying for a solution to a deep problem, the restoration of a relationship, salvation from intense loneliness, abandonment, rejection, or some other painful problem. Sometimes it seems impossible to breathe, let alone sleep.

The psalmist has been there. And he acknowledged God's rescue.

The psalmist was battling all kinds of worries. Perhaps that sounds familiar. Yet, God reached out in response to his need.

There is hope. And there is life. But it's not found internally; there you'll find only more sadness and anxiety. It's found only in God. He is poised to rescue you and relieve your pain.

He holds the deepest part of the earth in his hands, and the mountain peaks belong to him. The ocean is the Lord's because he made it, and with his own hands he formed the dry land.

—Psalm 95:4–5

The deepest and the highest. The seas and the deserts. And everything in between.

All of it rests in the hands of the One who created it all: God Himself. It all belongs to Him because He made it. And everything that transpires in every area of the earth does so under His watchful eyes, under His personal control.

Truly, God is great. Imagine if you can the power, the intelligence, and the creativity necessary to put together the world.

This is the God who knows and loves you. The God who is worthy of your love and worship today. The God who can be trusted wherever you find yourself in His creation today.

DAY 236

Bow down and worship the LORD our Creator! The LORD is our God, and we are his people, the sheep he takes care of in his own pasture.

—*Psalm 95:6–7*

What do you suppose sheep think about their shepherd? Do they appreciate his watchfulness and protection from both elements and natural enemies? Do they thank him for providing the food they need every day? Do they wonder how he could be so wise and caring? Do they enjoy following him wherever he leads them? Or do they take him for granted and merely get through life as sheep?

These are thought-provoking questions. Because we believers are really sheep, and God is our Shepherd.

Sheep are simpleminded and lazy creatures. They must have guidance, or they would perish on their own.

We are very much the same. The psalmist urges us to appreciate our Shepherd, to worship Him, to give Him our lives. Because our lives are already His.

Sing a new song to the LORD! Everyone on this earth, sing praises to the LORD, sing and praise his name. Day after day announce, "The LORD has saved us!"

—Psalm 96:1–2

Sing to the Lord! Open your mouth and pour out praise to Him!

It's a new song, fresh, meaningful—and yet it's as ancient as time itself. And you have the privilege of singing it today.

Think of your life as a song—the emotions you carry as major and minor chords, the words you speak as the lyrics, the actions you perform as musical movements.

What is your song telling others? Is it primarily a minor key? Is it something others like to listen to?

The psalmist urges God's people to sing the truth of God, the good news of His salvation, day after day.

May your life be a winsome song, a tune that offers up praise to God.

Everyone on earth, now tremble and worship the LORD, majestic and holy.

—Psalm 96:9

You see something so beautiful, and you shudder.

You fear something so deeply, and you shake.

What's the difference? And how does either apply to the God you love?

The psalmist admonishes us to worship God in His majestic holiness. In the clear, pure light of His holiness, all our need is exposed. Our sin is revealed. Our true nature is known. And that can be scary.

But God sees us as clean and pure and holy in Jesus Christ. He sees us as His children. He sees us as beautiful.

And that realization is wonderful. When it reaches down to the core of our being and warms us with its truth, we may shudder with emotion.

Understand who God is. Accept His forgiving love. And tremble before Him.

Tell the heavens and the earth to be glad and celebrate! Command the ocean to roar with all of its creatures and the fields to rejoice with all of their crops. Then every tree in the forest will sing joyful songs to the LORD.

—Psalm 96:11–13

Why are we so quiet when it comes to acknowledging God and His creative work in our lives? After all, creation around us sings. Day after day, night after night, the ocean, the trees, the rocks, the fields, the skies all point majestically, though wordlessly, to the One who is over all.

We can tune in to what they are saying. We can hear the starry skies worship, the earth sing, the ocean roar, the fields and trees whisper and murmur. All creatures of the earth voice their joy over life and creation.

It takes a spiritual ear to hear such things. But developing an ear like that aids us in our own praise. Witnessing the free-spirited joy of creation over its existence can kindle our own thanks to the One who gave us life and helps us live it.

DAY 240

Light is sown for the righteous, And gladness for the upright in heart. Rejoice in the LORD, you righteous, And give thanks at the remembrance of His holy name.

—Psalm 97:11–12 NKJV

God's light pours down over us, even in the darkness. It illuminates the thoughts of our minds, the emotions of the heart. It brightens our pathway. But we must open our eyes to see it. And when we do, if we walk righteously and honestly before God, we will be glad.

God sows His light in our souls as a farmer sows seeds in the ground. The seeds take root, send forth tender shoots, grow strong and green and fresh, and ultimately provide fruit.

The light of God's Word does the same in our lives. Welcome the light. Open the windows of your spirit to it

Let Him plant the seeds of truth. Water them with your fervency and hope. It all leads to a glad heart, a rejoicing spirit, a thankful soul.

The LORD has shown the nations that he has the power to save and to bring justice.

—*Psalm 98:2*

After the season of Christmas, Christians celebrate the Epiphany—the appearance of Jesus Christ in the world, the Light shining to all the nations.

He is here; He has announced Himself; He has shown Himself to all who would see. And there can be no doubt about who He is and what He has come to do.

He is your Savior. You have come to know His salvation, provided by the Son of God through His sacrificial death on the cross.

It is no secret to anyone who would pursue the truth. His righteousness is openly shown. But His self-revelation calls for a response.

He stands before humanity as the One who has come as the salvation of God. He offers Himself freely to all. You have accepted His gift. Now you stand among the nations. Will you, too, make known His salvation today?

Command the ocean to roar with all of its creatures, and the earth to shout with all of its people. Order the rivers to clap their hands, and all of the hills to sing together. Let them worship the LORD! He is coming to judge everyone on the earth, and he will be honest and fair.

—Psalm 98:7–9

The Lord is coming to earth again: this time in judgment. Judgment is often equated in our minds with punishment.

Why, then, is the ocean "with all of its creatures" roaring with joy? Why are the rivers applauding in victory and the hills exuding joy before the coming Lord?

They know instinctively that His judgment is pure and righteous and absolutely fair. He judges without malice or deference. He is God.

You can await His judgment with the same knowledge and acceptance. For your sins have already been judged in Jesus Christ.

You are our mighty King, a lover of fairness, who sees that justice is done everywhere in Israel.

—Psalm 99:4

Bur that's not fair! I have my rights!" How often have you heard such sentiments? How often have you uttered them?

It seems justice is in the eye of the beholder. As though the world revolved around what is right for me, what I think is best, what's in my best interests, what I have coming to me.

It's easy to fall in that trap because we're surrounded by it in the world in which we live. But there is only one "right" thing, and only one kind of justice will stand. God's.

As the Ruler of the universe, He has established the foundations, the rules if you will, of life in that universe. He is the final Arbiter of fairness.

As His followers, we can yield to His justice because we know Him and trust Him. And we know He is mighty enough to carry out His justice as he sees fit. We can leave everything in the hands of a loving, wise, and powerful God.

Our LORD and our God, you answered their prayers and forgave their sins, but when they did wrong, you punished them.

—Psalm 99:8

Israel had a direct pipeline to the living God. He even spoke to them in a pillar of cloud and fire (v. 7). At times, they listened and obeyed. At other times, they ignored and scoffed at His will. They even turned to false gods.

God remained their God. Despite their cold hearts and closed minds, He kept pursuing them. He kept loving them. He kept wooing them to return.

At the same time, He punished their misdeeds. Those punishments were the direct consequences of their hardened hearts. And through them all, God remained ready to answer their pleas for forgiveness.

He is the same God today. Though we may suffer the consequences of our sin, He loves us still. He accepts us always. He is our God forever.

You know the LORD is God! He created us, and we belong to him; we are his people, the sheep in his pasture.

—Psalm 100:3

There is a difference between knowledge and knowing something at the core of your being.

Your mind is filled with facts that you know. That is mere intellectual assent.

Contrast that with knowing something so deeply, trusting it so completely, that it becomes part of your life's foundation. Knowing the love of a friend is unshakable, no matter how foolishly you act. Knowing you are valuable and have much to contribute to the world around you. And above all, knowing that the Lord is God.

You know that. But does its truth form every thought you think, every breath you inhale, every step you take, every hug you give, every word you utter?

It can. And when it does, every thought, breath, step, hug, and word will be all the more meaningful, powerful, sweet, and fulfilling.

DAY 246

For the LORD is good; His mercy is everlasting, And
His truth endures to all generations.

—*Psalm 100:5 NKJV*

Goodness. Mercy. Truth. Three aspects of God
that can bring you a blessing of joy and fulfillment as you face the day.

You live in a world of badness, evil, and pain.
Of selfishness, judgmentalism, and strife. Of
falsehood, deceit, and treachery.

You're surrounded by the negatives continually, no matter where you go in the world. But
even in that context you can immerse yourself in
the holiness of God. Let His loving goodness,
mercy, and truth envelop you with their protection and perception.

So you can make your way through the darkened world with the light of God. It fills your
heart with purpose and joy. It shines through you
to illumine the dark corners with His truth. It
enables you to walk in serenity.

But only when you know it and accept it and
keep your eyes on it.

SEPTEMBER 2

DAY 247

Please help me learn to do the right thing, and I will be honest and fair in my own kingdom.

—Psalm 101:2

David the king made a commitment to live a life honoring the Lord who loved him. As the king, he pledged to act in a manner worthy of his calling. As a child of God, he pledged to live in the light that God shed on his path.

David's heart was in the right place. He wanted his life to reflect to the nations the glory of God. He yearned to do the Lord's will.

Certainly, David failed. He would be the first to admit his life was not perfect. And that may be the realization you need to struggle with today.

God does not demand perfection from His children. That's an impossible goal, and if it is ours, we will drive ourselves to distraction trying to live up to a false standard.

Our perfection is in Christ, who paid for our sins and intercedes for us now. The perfection God desires is our willingness to do His will.

SEPTEMBER 3

I refuse to be corrupt or to take part in anything crooked, and I won't be dishonest or deceitful.

—Psalm 101:3–4

Life is full of influences. Your parents. Television. Your spouse. Music. Your friends. The Bible. Your pastor. Your Sunday school teacher. Magazines. Prayer. The news media. Books. Your environment. Your upbringing. Your extended family. Your coworkers. The list continues; add your own.

How does each one influence the way you think, the negative feelings you struggle with, the positive emotions that give wing to your soul, the words you say, the actions you perform?

Now ask yourself, What seems out of balance? What negative thoughts, feelings, and actions am I struggling with? What positive thoughts, feelings, and actions would I like to strengthen and expand? In terms of influences, what needs to change in order for that to happen?

DAY 249

No one who cheats or lies will have a position in my royal court.

—Psalm 101:7

As the leader of his land, David made a commitment to walk a straight line, keep a pure heart, and maintain a clean slate with God. Part of that commitment involved being careful about those he associated with—friends, aides, advisors. He said anyone who acted deceitfully or told lies would not be part of his life. He couldn't afford the moral distractions.

You may be aware of another's negative influence on your life. A friend, even a close family member, who uses you, deceives you, lies to you or others in order to get what he wants.

There comes a point when you have to say that enough is enough. Because the false words and deceitful deeds of others can have a subtly insidious effect on your words and deeds.

Be aware of how others behave and speak. Watch and listen with spiritual eyes and ears. Ask yourself whether you need to join David in his commitment.

He shall regard the prayer of the destitute, And shall not despise their prayer.

—Psalm 102:17 NKJV

The world may ignore destitute people. But God doesn't.

The psalmist finds himself in a tough situation. In pain, alone, and terribly needy, he considers himself totally lacking in everything. And while acknowledging that, he also realizes that God is the God of the destitute as well—whether they are destitute monetarily, spiritually, or emotionally.

Jesus said the poor in spirit were blessed of God. Perhaps because they reached the end of their own resources and were forced to rely on God.

You may not be homeless, but you may feel needy today. If so, pray in confidence that you love a God who will hear you.

Then be aware of the many people around you who are destitute as well and may need some directions from a friend. Point them to God.

Future generations must also praise the LORD.
—*Psalm 102:18*

Did you know you were in the Bible? You're part of the future generations for whom the psalmist wrote this poem of praise. His desire when he wrote these words hundreds and hundreds of years ago was to point you to the same God he worshiped.

Today, you can fulfill this ancient prophecy. And praise the Lord.

Praise Him for teaching you His way. Praise Him for friends and loved ones. Praise Him for His creation. Praise Him for a living, growing relationship with Him through Jesus. Praise Him for the quickening, empowering Spirit who dwells within. Praise Him for creativity and beauty. Praise Him for achievement and growth. Praise Him for the specific joys of your day. Praise the Lord!

From his holy temple, the LORD looked down at the earth. He listened to the groans of prisoners, and he rescued everyone who was doomed to die.

—Psalm 102:19–20

Does God feel distant to you? Aloof? So far above that you can't see Him, let alone feel His presence?

The psalmist sends this word of encouragement: God is looking down from His heavenly dwelling place. He sees the entire earth and every soul dwelling on it. He hears the groaning of those imprisoned by chains or fear or depression or confusion. He acts to rescue those who have been sentenced to eternal death.

He may be removed in one sense, but He is totally present with you in another.

If you feel imprisoned by an emotion, a person, an event, or a problem, don't be afraid to groan. He hears you. He sees you. He knows you. He loves you. He frees you.

They will all disappear and wear out like clothes. You change them, as you would a coat, but you last forever. You are always the same. Years cannot change you.

—Psalm 102:26–27

The heavens and the earth. They seem ancient to us. Solid. Unyielding. Irreplaceable. To our small minds, with our brief lives, they seem to have no beginning and should have no end.

But the psalmist dismisses that notion with a few words: "They will all disappear." All creation will grow old. Like out-of-fashion, torn, or fading clothing that you toss away, they will be changed. Even the heavens and the earth!

But God, the Creator, is distinct from His creation. He will endure. He made the heavens and the earth, and He will change them. He is always the same. His years have no end.

You have an all-powerful God you can turn to at any moment, no matter what's happening in your changing world. A God who will understand and who will act to make things right.

With all my heart I praise the LORD, and with all that I am I praise his holy name!

—*Psalm 103:1*

Every organ. Every cell. Every neuron. Every molecule. Every part of your being praising God. Honoring Him. Glorifying Him. And acknowledging Him as the God of the universe.

Is that happening today? Maybe it doesn't feel like it. Even searching down deep inside, it's hard to find a part of you that's thankful, joyful, or hopeful.

But that part is there. And if you can focus on it—let it out, let it grow, let it sing—it can start influencing all the other parts of who you are.

How do you do that? For starters, recite this verse. Listen to what you're saying. Think about the words. Think about the One you're talking about.

Let the fears melt. Let the anxieties crumble. Let the frustrations dissolve.

Praise the Lord.

With all my heart I praise the LORD! I will never forget how kind he has been. The LORD forgives our sins, heals us when we are sick, and protects us from death. His kindness and love are a crown on our heads.

—Psalm 103:2–4

As you praise and honor God, remember all His benefits to you.

He forgives your sins. Through His Son, Jesus Christ, He has satisfied His demands for holiness, enabling you to enter His presence cleansed through His work on the cross.

He heals your diseases. That may not mean you won't catch cold or even contract a fatal disease. You may. But you can count on Him to heal your soul in the process.

He protects you from death. As His child, you are aimed toward heaven. Your destruction is no longer a possibility.

He crowns you with kindness and love. Your life overflows with His blessings.

DAY 256

[He] satisfies your mouth with good things, So that your youth is renewed like the eagle's.

—*Psalm 103:5 NKJV*

The Lord gives you everything you need for your physical strength, enabling you to stay hearty and healthy and active.

In the Lord's Prayer, Jesus instructed us to pray, "Give us this day our daily bread" (Matt. 6:11 NKJV). That simple request would help us keep in mind that even the essentials of life are given to us from God's hand. He is the One who gives us the food to eat. It's easy to lose sight of that since we pay someone else for it.

Still, God is ultimately the source of all life and of everything that supports it.

Today, think of the good things you enjoy eating. The times you've shared with others over a meal. All that is a major part of life. Don't take it for granted. At every meal, pause and thank God for His provision of all good things. Then start soaring like a strong eagle.

SEPTEMBER 12

He doesn't punish us as our sins deserve.
—Psalm 103:10

God is holy. His holiness requires Him to deal justly with sinful humans. But His mercy has provided the means to satisfy His justice and give us freedom from sin's penalty.

That mercy was poured out upon us through Jesus Christ. Thanks to his self-sacrifice, we can enter into an eternal relationship with the Father.

It didn't have to be that way. God had every right to let us wallow in our sin and wickedness and self-absorption until we self-destructed.

The psalmist points out this truth. If God had truly dealt with us as we deserved, we would have been zapped into oblivion long ago.

Not that we should disparage ourselves over this. That's precisely the point: God saw fit to reach out to us in grace. We can receive that. We can accept the absolution of our sins. We can trust that He has forgiven and forgotten. We are free.

How far has the LORD taken our sins from us? Farther than the distance from east to west!

—Psalm 103:12

God's forgiveness of us knows no limits or boundaries.

Think about the world. Trace a line on a globe from where you live northward. You'll soon hit the North Pole. Keep going, and you begin moving south.

There is an end to north. Likewise there is an end to south.

Now put your finger back where you live. Move it eastward. Keep going. You'll circle the globe, and you'll still be moving east. There is no end to east or west.

And that's how far God has taken our sins. It's an infinite distance.

Your sins have been removed. You need not live under their burden. If you are struggling with guilt over the sins that plagued you in the past, it's time to let go.

If you need to work through them, seek help. If a pattern of sin still exists in your life, seek help. You are forgiven. God accepts you totally and loves you completely.

Just as parents are kind to their children, the LORD is kind to all who worship him, because he knows we are made of dust.

—Psalm 103:13–14

A child is sad over the loss of a broken toy. She grieves over a friend who moves away. He falls and skins his knee. She gets frustrated when she can't get the puzzle pieces to fit. He doesn't make the team. She has a fight with a friend who won't speak to her. A parent would look at these situations and offer consolation and encouragement.

And that's just what God the Father does for us if we'll run to His arms. He doesn't want perfection from us. He doesn't expect that we won't be sad or disappointed or hurting or frustrated or angry.

He understands how He made us: He knows that we are human. That means we will fail. That we will try to do things our own stubborn way. That we will lose control. That we will do foolish things. That we will never understand things completely.

When you hurt, run to your heavenly Daddy. Accept His loving care.

We humans are like grass or wild flowers that quickly bloom. But a scorching wind blows, and they quickly wither to be forever forgotten. The LORD is always kind to those who worship him, and he keeps his promises to their descendants.

—Psalm 103:15–17

David pictures human life as grass, as flowers of the field. Gorgeous and colorful and alive and flourishing—but then, with the blowing of the wind, they are gone.

And yet, as transitory as life is, God is precisely the opposite. He has always been and will always be. His mercy is forever extended to those who worship Him. His righteousness carries on from generation to generation of those who follow Him.

Your life will end on earth. But it will never end in His presence.

The legacy you leave behind on earth to those who follow you can be glorious as well. A legacy of abiding faith in an unchanging God.

All of you mighty angels, who obey God's commands, come and praise your LORD! All of you thousands who serve and obey God, come and praise your LORD! All of God's creation and all that he rules, come and praise your LORD! With all my heart I praise the LORD!

—*Psalm 103:20–22*

All the angels who populate heaven and surround God's throne are praising Him. All the hosts of heaven—all spiritual beings in God's dwelling place—are honoring Him with their worship. All the works of His hands—all things in the physical universe He created—are glorifying His name. And finally, your heart is invited to join in.

The mind cannot fathom such an uproarious, joyful, and honorable celebration of God's goodness. And yet, you can be part of it right now.

Lift your cares. Let loose your burdens. Pause in the busyness of your day and praise the Lord. You may even hear the angels singing with you.

He lays the beams of His upper chambers in the waters, Who makes the clouds His chariot, Who walks on the wings of the wind, Who makes His angels spirits, His ministers a flame of fire.

—*Psalm 104:3–4 NKJV*

God establishes the rain that waters and nourishes the earth in the clouds of the sky. He moves around and above us on a chariot of clouds, "on the wings of the wind."

He summons and sends out His angelic ministers to work His will in the earth—protecting, guiding, providing.

He is working continually, establishing His will, answering prayers, touching lives, healing sick hearts. Even in your life.

He is all-powerful, all-present, all-knowing, all-loving. And He is acting on your behalf.

Acknowledge His sovereignty. Applaud His power. Accept His gracious work in your life. Look at the sky today, and know He is there. And everywhere. And even in your heart.

From your home above you send rain on the hills and water the earth.

—*Psalm 104:13*

Have you walked through orchards stretching over lush hills? Have you picked berries from fruit-burdened bushes? Have you driven by miles of cornfields? The abundance of the earth can be overwhelming. It sparks praise for God's amazing provision for His children. We are satisfied with the goodness of His hands.

And yet, we are shaken from our grateful reverie with the realization that countless millions of souls on earth are hungry for even the basics of life. Their lands are desolate. They suffer at the hands of ruthless people. Their plight is heartbreaking.

God has provided more than enough for the earth and everyone on it.

There are ways that the needs can be met. But it takes action. Hard work. A strong voice. Determination. And a caring heart.

And you can pray for those who have yet to taste satisfaction with the fruit of God's hands.

DAY 264

You let the earth produce grass for cattle, plants for
our food, wine to cheer us up, olive oil for our skin,
and grain for our health.

—Psalm 104:14–15

These verses list some of the most common elements of life—grass for cows to eat, plants for
humans to use for food and beauty, anointing
oil, grain.

All have important benefits that help us live.
By keeping the cows happy, we have milk and
meat. From plants, we have nutritious food. Oil
is for grooming and fragrance. Grain is an essen-
tial for our meals.

Simple. Straightforward. And necessary for
life.

But how often do we take notice of God's
hand behind each of these blessings? For He is
the One who causes each one; and without them,
we could very well perish.

Take note of the simple things in life today.
Refuse to take anything for granted. Appreciate
the Source. And praise Him for all the blessings
of your life. Where would you be without them?

SEPTEMBER 20

DAY 265

Our Lord, by your wisdom you made so many things; the whole earth is covered with your living creatures. But what about the ocean so big and wide? It is alive with creatures, large and small.

—*Psalm 104:24–25*

Plants, animals, insects, fish—all kinds of living things fill this earth.

The psalmist praises the infinitely creative God, whose works are many and varied. God made every single organism of them in His immeasurable wisdom. Each has a purpose in itself. Each can bring us pleasure through its existence. It's all part of His incredibly complex master plan.

Admittedly, too many species are dying. That's not the earth's fault or the Creator's. As stewards of the earth and all that God created on it, we humans aren't doing as good a job as we could be.

God owns it all—yet He has left it all in our hands to care for.

Will you take seriously the fact that everything on this earth is precious to God because He created it?

SEPTEMBER 21

DAY 266

All of these depend on you to provide them with food, and you feed each one with your own hand, until they are full.

—Psalm 104:27–28

Even the creatures of earth know who gives them the food they need to survive. They depend on Him. They gather in what He gives them.

The living things of earth and sea and sky don't worry about their next meal. They don't drive themselves to distraction if they feel they don't have enough and won't get enough.

Jesus also pointed to the birds of the air and the flowers of the field, which worried not about their clothing or food or other necessities of life.

They lived in trust. They accepted the gifts that life gave them. They grew steadily.

Let them teach you the simple lesson of trust in God's provision. He holds all things in His hands. And those hands He opens to any need.

He knows what you need today. Depend on Him to provide it.

You created all of them by your Spirit, and you give new life to the earth.

—Psalm 104:30

The Spirit of God hovered over the face of the newly created earth and went to work.

God reached into the clay and formed the living things. It must have been a delight for Him to populate the planet so abundantly.

The foliage grew; the creatures propagated and spread throughout the planet. And in so doing, the earth itself was given new life.

He re-creates the same scenario with every individual who trusts Him. He sends the Spirit, and we are re-created. Our souls are renewed. Our spirits are given life.

Life. Abundance. Activity. Renewal. Fulfillment. Joy. All can become ongoing aspects of your life in the wake of the Spirit of God working in and through you. Are you experiencing them? Are you receiving the Spirit sent forth on your behalf? God's life-giving power is at work in the world. And it can be at work within you as well.

Glory in His holy name; Let the hearts of those rejoice who seek the LORD! Seek the LORD and His strength; Seek His face evermore!

—*Psalm 105:3–4 NKJV*

There is a certain kind of person who can revel in the light of God's countenance. Whose face shines with the promise of life in the Spirit. Whose heart rejoices continually in the work of God in life. Who glories in His name as His child, as His heir forever.

The kind of person who enjoys life like that is a seeker. She seeks the Lord and His strength. He yearns to be in the light of His presence at all times.

How do you get to that place? By taking the first step. By turning your face toward Him, your heart toward His Word, your mind toward His truth, your body away from the things that distract you. Run after the Lord; you need not run far, for He is waiting. Seek and you will find. And in the finding, you will rejoice.

DAY 269

When the Lord rescued his chosen people from Egypt, they celebrated with songs. The Lord gave them the land and everything else the nations had worked for. He did this so that his people would obey all of his laws. Shout praises to the LORD!

—Psalm 105:43–45

After years of slavery in Egypt, God brought His people out with joy and freedom. Through Abraham, He had made them His possession. And He was giving them a new possession: the Promised Land.

God intended His people to live lives of such joy, honesty, and love that He could be seen through them to the world around them. They were His channel for blessing the world. They would show humanity the difference He made in life.

Often, it didn't work out that way. Too often, people who really didn't know God held sway over the actions of the nation.

How much like Israel are you living today? How much like a child of God?

Remember me, LORD, when you show kindness by saving your people. Let me prosper with the rest of your chosen ones, as they celebrate with pride because they belong to you.

—Psalm 106:4–5

You are part of a larger organism, a single limb or organ in a vast body.

It is the body of Christ. And with your salvation, you became part of this fellowship forever. What happens in and to the body of Christ affects you. You cannot truly experience personal fulfillment and happiness unless the body is in good health, working as it was designed to work.

The psalmist recognized this truth as part of the chosen people, the nation Israel. God's favor was poured out upon that body, and in experiencing it as part of the whole, the psalmist would find purpose and joy individually.

You're part of the body of Christ. You're part of a local fellowship of believers. What part are you playing in each? How is the health of the body affecting you?

We and our ancestors have sinned terribly.
—*Psalm 106:6*

It's one thing to admit that you have sinned. It's another thing altogether to take responsibility for the entire group of which you're a part—and even those who preceded you. It takes a humble heart, a realistic mind, and an obedient spirit to acknowledge what's gone wrong and why.

The psalmist admitted that he was just as much a sinner as his ancestors who truly rebelled against God. He didn't blame his sinfulness on those past acts. He didn't avoid his personal responsibility.

You can blame your family for your character flaws. You can point to the environment in which you grew up. You can even let yourself off the hook because you're a faulty human being. But it's also important to take responsibility for your faults. And to clean the slate with your loving, forgiving Father.

When they were in Egypt, they paid no attention to your marvelous deeds or your wonderful love. And they turned against you at the Red Sea. But you were true to your name, and you rescued them to prove how mighty you are.

—Psalm 106:7–8

One of the most difficult things in life as human beings is admitting that we don't necessarily know what's best. That doing things our own way can cause more problems.

One of the easiest things in life is looking at other people and seeing those truths clearly, for instance, the Israelites in the Old Testament. We can't understand their disobedience. Yet they displayed it freely in God's face. In our own minds, we're much different from them. But perhaps God sees things differently.

He had a purpose in mind with the Israelites: He let them get so desperately stuck that He could display His redemptive power in their lives and demonstrate the kind of God He is to the world at large. He does that in individual lives as well.

DAY 273

You answered their prayers when they were in trouble. You kept your agreement and were so merciful.
—*Psalm 106:44–45*

God's Word is unbreakable.

With Israel He made a covenant to be their God. Unfortunately, they didn't keep their end of the deal. In fact, they went off in an entirely different direction, into the realm of sin, degradation, and idolatry. And they stayed there until they realized what a terrible mess they had gotten themselves into. And so they cried unto God.

He heard them. He kept His agreement. His mercy overshadowed His justice. His forgiving heart held sway over His righteousness.

And that can give you hope, too. When you are in pain—even pain caused by your stubborn self-will—He will hear you. He will remember you. He will reach out to you in mercy.

Save us, LORD God! Bring us back from among the nations. Let us celebrate and shout in praise of your holy name.

—Psalm 106:47

Thank God, we don't have to earn God's favor or work for His salvation. We'd never make it.

The Israelites acknowledged that. They had self-destructed, ending up scattered and lost, removed from their homeland, distanced from their heavenly Father. They reached the point of crying, "Save us!" They longed to be regathered from the Gentile nations to which they had been exiled.

They could rely only on His forgiveness and love, not on what they had accomplished. They pledged only to thank Him and praise Him for His works.

And that's about as much as we can offer, too. That's more than enough for Him.

When you find yourself scattered and lost, God will hear your cry. He's just waiting for you to want to come back to Him.

DAY 275

You should praise the LORD for his love and for the wonderful things he does for all of us. To everyone who is thirsty, he gives something to drink; to everyone who is hungry, he gives good things to eat.

—*Psalm 107:8–9*

A dissatisfied soul can eat away at the core. We hunger for acceptance and love. We yearn for someone to want us. We long to be filled with serenity and hope. We work ourselves into a frenzy seeking to fill the emptiness and loneliness, and find ourselves so deeply needy that nothing seems to work.

Friends can help, loved ones can offer support, but the longing soul refuses to be satisfied. The emptiness is a vast, dark, cold ocean within that seems impossible to fill.

When we reach our limits, there is only one way out: to turn to God with our open, empty hands. Only God can satisfy; only God can fill. His resources are without limit. He desires to give us an abundance.

Some of you were prisoners suffering in deepest darkness and bound by chains, because you had rebelled against God Most High and refused his advice.

—Psalm 107:10–11

We know what we need. We know how to get it. Or so we think.

Our minds dwell on our pains and problems, trying to figure out how to rid our lives of them so we can be happy and fulfilled. We fill our lives with people or things to soothe the pain. This is rebellion. It may not feel like it, but it is. It's turning to ourselves, other people, or things, apart from God, to solve our problems.

It's not God's way. So it won't work. We find ourselves in darkness, the soul facing death, tied up in our affliction as in bonds of iron. Rather than seek God's counsel or ask for His empowering Spirit, we ignore Him and His gracious offer to help.

Soften your heart. Open your soul to heaven. Stop striving to fill the emptiness on your own terms. Look to Him for the word you need to give insights and answers.

DAY 277

He brought you out of the deepest darkness and broke your chains.

—*Psalm 107:14*

The darkness can suffocate at times. The pain can overwhelm. The soul can yearn for freedom from the pit of despair, freedom even in the embrace of death.

In the depths, hope seems impossible. The light of life is but a dim memory, taunting us, making the pain only that much deeper.

If that's where you are today, force yourself to open your eyes. Look around. See the thin ray of God's love coming through the clouds of heaven? It's there. The clouds are moving. It may be some time before the sky is clear again, but they are moving.

Feel the chains of fear and pain loosening? They are. God is breaking them. It may be only one link at a time, but He is breaking them.

The psalmist knew that God would do that because He had done it in the past.

He is still doing it today. He is doing it in your life.

OCTOBER 3

You were in serious trouble, but you prayed to the LORD, and he rescued you. He made the storm stop and the sea be quiet. You were happy because of this, and he brought you to the port where you wanted to go.

—Psalm 107:28–30

This is the way it is supposed to work: We pray to God in our trouble; He rescues us. Sometimes it doesn't work. Because we get absorbed in our pain. Or we try to fix it ourselves. Or we don't think to pray to God. Sometimes it doesn't work but never because God isn't able. He is working if we are willing to let Him. The work may be long and painful, but it is unfolding in its perfect time.

The storms of life are calmed at His command; the waves are stilled in the presence of the Spirit of peace. And when the storms are calmed over the waters of life, He can guide us to safe harbor.

God is sovereign over the storm. He is sovereign over your life. Seek the quiet and calm through Him. He will guide you to a haven of safety.

DAY 279

When you are suffering and in need, he will come to your rescue, and your families will grow as fast as a herd of sheep. You will see this because you obey the LORD, but everyone who is wicked will be silenced.

—*Psalm 107:41–42*

God can shape universes and worlds, change their courses, bring them into and out of existence. His power is infinite. So the power needed to lift those who are needy in spirit, mind, emotions, and body to a higher plane is nothing to Him.

Any who need help can receive it from Him. He can rescue them from their suffering, says the psalmist. He can gather them and their loved ones together like a flock, and shepherd them.

You can see it happening in others' lives. Sometimes it's harder to see it in your own. But if your eyes are open and clear to the work of God, you will see it. And rejoice. If you need to feel part of God's flock, if you need to see God working, just ask Him for it.

OCTOBER 5

Our God, may you be honored above the heavens;
may your glory be seen everywhere on earth. Answer
my prayers and use your powerful arm to give us victory. Then the people you love will be safe.

—Psalm 108:5–6

Life is too busy, isn't it? So many distractions
vie for your time and energy. You need time with
God. Sometimes you need to force yourself to sit
quietly, to think meditatively, to turn your attention to God. When you do, you can experience a
restoration of the soul that only He can give.

Because only then can you see God apart from
the distractions that cloud your vision. You can
see Him as exalted and glorious, powerful and
loving. And only then can He really hear you.
And in hearing, deliver you. And in delivering,
save you.

For your soul's sake, spend some time today
worshiping God.

You are the one who gives us victory and crushes our enemies.

—*Psalm 108:13*

There is no better feeling than experiencing personal victory. Reveling in freedom from a troublesome problem or a deep emotional pain. Making a major step of progress in becoming a more whole and healthy person.

The enemies of your life are likely not armed warriors from opposing kingdoms, as the psalmist faced. Nevertheless, you do have enemies. Negative thoughts and attitudes, painful past experiences, others in your life who demand more than you can give—the list could be endless.

How do you deal with the enemies? By facing them. Working through them. Accepting them. Learning from them. Letting them go.

Reduced to those words, it sounds quite easy. You know it's not.

And it can work only if you permit God to give you the victory.

Destructive and deceitful lies are told about me. . . .
I had pity and prayed for my enemies, but their
words to me were harsh and cruel.

—Psalm 109:2, 4

Sometimes we can feel suffocated by the evil in
the world around us. Constantly, we hear things
that tear down the God of the universe and His
people, His will, and His ways. We take the
charges personally.

In a culture increasingly hostile to the things
of God, it's easy to slide into an angry, fearful,
harsh, and strident manner of attack. And that
will get us nowhere.

The psalmist acknowledged that the wicked of
the world will always tear down what's good and
right and godly in it. His response to them was
different, however: He reached out in love. He
prayed for them. That's the way of the child of
God in a world of evil.

But nothing changed. The wicked remained
his accusers. Their words still hurt.

Keep at it. Keep praying. Keep trusting God.
And God will triumph in the end.

Be true to your name, LORD God! Show your great kindness and rescue me. I am poor and helpless, and I have lost all hope.

—Psalm 109:21–22

Because you are a child of God, His name is at stake when it comes to what happens to you.

David the psalmist beseeched God to take care of him, to deal with the things that troubled him. David claimed the name of God and was claimed by God as His own.

So David's defeat would reflect on God's name. If he were unable to deal with the problems that perplexed him and bound him, God's lovingkindness could be called into question.

David was hurting. Empty. Needy. He had lost all hope. You know that feeling. You may be experiencing it right now. Call on the name of the Lord, the name that can be trusted.

Please help me, LORD God! Come and save me because of your love. Let others know that you alone have saved me.

—Psalm 109:26–27

In desperation, David cried out to God: "Help me! . . . Save me!" He knew God would hear. And that He would act according to His mercy—abundantly, powerfully, lovingly.

But David wasn't asking God to rescue him simply to be rescued. He wanted his deliverance to be recognized for what it was: an act of God.

So often we focus so intently on the problem at hand that it's difficult to turn to God and ask for help. And if we are able to do that, it's often difficult to see how God could use our desperation—and our deliverance—to affect someone else.

Save me, Lord, that others may know it's Your hand at work—that they can see that You have done it. It wasn't my success, my power, my superiority that handled it. It was You and You alone.

I don't care if they curse me, as long as you bless me. You will make my enemies fail when they attack, and you will make me glad to be your servant.

—Psalm 109:28

If we sense the blessing of God in our lives, our enemies can curse us all they want. Their curses mean nothing in the light of God's word.

David asked God to make his enemies fail while making him glad. And that's a natural response. You've probably prayed something similar.

God certainly will cause His children to rejoice, but whether He answers in the way we want the prayer for failure regarding those who oppose Him is another matter. In truth, their foolishness brings its own failure.

Those who speak ill of you or seek to oppose you have no power over you unless you give it to them. Instead, seek God's power. Ask for His blessing. And nothing anyone else does will matter.

DAY 286

The LORD said to my Lord, "Sit at my right side, until I make your enemies into a footstool for you."
—*Psalm 110:1*

The New Testament writers often used this psalm of David in reference to the Messiah, Jesus, the Son of God.

In it, he wrote that the Lord God spoke to "my Lord," referring to the Messiah and using language that indicates deity. And the Lord God invited the Messiah to sit at His right side. That was the place of supreme authority. One who sat at the earthly king's right side was empowered to rule over the realm on his behalf. And this is the place the New Testament tells us from which Christ rules, even today (Acts 5:31; Rom. 8:34; Heb. 1:13; 10:12–13).

The Lord God revealed that the Messiah will rule over creation "until I make your enemies into a footstool." Ultimately, God will reign over all. Even now, His plan is unfolding. And you are part of it.

Your people shall be volunteers In the day of Your power; In the beauties of holiness, from the womb of the morning, You have the dew of Your youth.

—Psalm 110:3 NKJV

As the Messiah rules in the heavenlies over us and all of creation, His people will willingly serve Him and gloriously triumph in His power.

His people will shine beautifully in His holiness, for His righteousness has cleansed them and made them new. They have come from "the womb of the morning"—they are born again, embarking on a new beginning.

The Messiah will forever be young, vibrant, fresh. And because that is so, His people can experience the same newness of life. He continually makes things new, enabling us to grow and mature, to become healthier and holier humans.

Can your relationship with God and His Son be characterized as willing, beautiful, new, vibrant? Ask Him for it, and wait for His answer.

My Lord is at your right side, and when he gets angry he will crush the other kings. He will judge the nations and crack their skulls, leaving piles of dead bodies all over the earth.

—Psalm 110:5–6

While we consider the majesty and glory of the ruling Messiah at the right side of the Father, a jarring counterpoint comes into play in David's psalm today. It is a picture of judgment and death. And it is so matter-of-fact that it may surprise us.

But this is the way it is. In the end God will not tolerate evil. At His appointed time, His wrath will be given full vent. The wicked will receive everything they have so justly deserved. And it is not a pretty picture.

You, however, as a child of God—fear not. The day of judgment will be undertaken on your behalf.

God is holy and just. He is loving and merciful. He wills that no one would perish. But His holiness and justice will ultimately have their way.

The works of the LORD are great, Studied by all who have pleasure in them. His work is honorable and glorious, And His righteousness endures forever.

—*Psalm 111:2–3 NKJV*

We are surrounded by the works of the Lord. Outside us. And within us.

When we sense them consciously, a spark ignites our hearts. We may utter a word of praise. Our spirits may be lifted momentarily with the realization that something indeed has come from God's hand. And then we move on with our lives.

The psalmist instead invites us to spend some time thinking about God's great works. To study them. Reflect on them. And thereby enhance our pleasure over them. Whatever the work may be, we can see His honor in it. His glory. His righteousness. His everlastingness.

You are surrounded by God's works. See them? Realize what they are. Ascribe them to Him. Take pleasure in them. Learn from them.

He has made His wonderful works to be remembered; The LORD is gracious and full of compassion.

—Psalm 111:4 NKJV

The psalmist has reminded us to study God's works (v. 2). Now he recommends that we remember them as well.

That is God's purpose for His wonderful works: that we see them, know them, ponder them, and remember them. That we amass in our minds a collection of memories of His actions in our lives on our behalf. That we turn to those memories and draw strength and confidence whenever we feel weak and despairing. That we remind ourselves from them that He is "gracious and full of compassion." That we share them with our fellow travelers to give them encouragement and hope as well.

But to accomplish all that, we must see His works for what they are—the God of the universe at work in the lives of His children. He is working. You are growing, maturing, progressing. Remember that.

The fear of the LORD is the beginning of wisdom; A good understanding have all those who do His commandments. His praise endures forever.

—Psalm 111:10 NKJV

The fear of the LORD." Unfortunately to many of us today, that phrase has a negative connotation.

When the Old Testament writers used the phrase "the fear of the LORD," they didn't see God's people cowering in fright, frozen with anxiety. Rather, they saw God's people kneeling in humility, revering and honoring the God who possesses all power over them.

The fear of the Lord is the basis of a true relationship with God. It describes a life that is accountable to God. A life that knows God's will and attempts to follow it in God's power.

The fear of the Lord is love and honor and worship. It is a realization of His ultimate parenthood in our lives.

A good man deals graciously and lends; He will guide his affairs with discretion. Surely he will never be shaken; The righteous will be in everlasting remembrance.

—Psalm 112:5–6 NKJV

One who has a steady walk with God "deals graciously" with others. Grace surrounds everything he does. Acceptance, mercy, and honesty abound toward others.

He "lends" to others. In other words, he is free with his possessions; he recognizes God's ownership of them, so they don't own him. Consequently, he is more than willing to share what he has.

He "will guide his affairs with discretion." He plans, he works, and he carries his plans out with wisdom without drawing attention to himself.

As a result of this kind of solid lifestyle, "he will never be shaken."

If that's not you today, accept the differences. Acknowledge your needs. Take it as a goal. And ask God's help to begin making it a reality in your life.

Bad news won't bother them; they have decided to trust the LORD.

—Psalm 112:7

People who walk closely, steadily with God do not fear the future.

Even when bad news comes, they can accept it. That doesn't mean they won't have emotions about it—sadness, anger, even despair.

But they know there is no need to fear, even in the face of disaster, because they trust God.

They know God is in control of all things. God can work all things for the good. So when even terrible circumstances erupt around them, their immediate reaction is to jump into God's arms and let Him carry them.

Today, you may be fearing some impending bad news. You may not know where your life is heading—where you'll be working or living to-morrow. You have a great opportunity to trust God.

No one can compare with the LORD our God. His throne is high above, and he looks down to see the heavens and the earth.

—Psalm 113:5–6

When you think about God as the Sovereign of the universe, high and lifted up, the One whose "throne is high above," you may feel that you need binoculars to see Him. Or even a telescope.

He can seem removed, aloof. After all, He has a whole universe to run. What difference can your life make to Him?

But the Scripture reminds you time and again that God is only a prayer away. Reach out to Him, and you will find Him.

The psalmist acknowledged that God dwells on high, and yet He "looks down to see the heavens and the earth." In other words, He keeps His eyes on us all the time.

Yes, He could be removed. We could be beneath His very notice. Thank God, He chooses to get involved with us.

God lifts the poor and needy from dust and ashes,
and he lets them take part in ruling his people.

—Psalm 113:7–8

You can't get any lower than the ash heap. If you're there, it means you've hit bottom. Which is good news because it means God has an opportunity to raise you up.

The psalmist declares that God can raise those who are poor and needy—physically, spiritually, or emotionally—from the depths and seat them with the rulers. And you can't get any higher than that.

Does that mean you can expect instantaneous relief from the dust of your life?

No. The psalmist gives no clue as to how long this process of being lifted up can be. Sometimes it may happen quickly. Or it may take an entire lifetime. Or you may never experience the heights until you're with God in heaven. Even so, you can trust God that it is happening at whatever speed He deems best.

We don't deserve praise! The LORD alone deserves all of the praise, because of his love and faithfulness.

—Psalm 115:1

We take a step forward and give ourselves a pat on the back. We stand up for ourselves and applaud. We work through a difficult relationship successfully and cheer our growth.

It's not wrong to feel good about ourselves and the progress we're making. We just need to be aware of who is empowering it.

Yes, we did it. We avoided the sin; we made a step of progress; we chose to be honest in the face of fear. But we couldn't have done it without God's mercy, without God's truth to guide us.

Give yourself a cheer, but recognize the Source of all good.

Give yourself a pat on the back, but give God the glory for what He has done to enable you to do what you have done.

Our God is in the heavens, doing as he chooses. The idols of the nations are made of silver and gold.

—*Psalm 115:3–4*

God is alive. He is in heaven. He is self-sufficient. He does whatever He pleases—because He is God.

He is the only God there is. In the psalmist's day, various groups of people had their own gods. Idols made of silver and gold. But they represented nothing of reality. They were pieces of dead sculpture. Which was tragic for those who worshiped them. The idols were totally without power, wisdom, or emotion of any kind. Empty, futile, worthless.

You may not worship an idol like that, but many similarly dead and powerless things can absorb attention and keep it from God.

Look to the Lord, the One who lives and reigns and works in your life. If you don't put your trust in Him, you have nothing to trust.

I love you, LORD! You answered my prayers. You paid attention to me, and so I will pray to you as long as I live.

—Psalm 116:1–2

You have a friend you can call at any hour and know you will be welcomed. A friend who will spend whatever time you need to talk. A friend who will listen to your pains and problems with compassion and understanding. A friend who will be there to support you when life's events seem to drag you down.

You may have a human friend of that nature. But you certainly have a heavenly One. The Lord God. He hears your prayers. He keeps His ear turned toward you. But even more, He acts on your behalf. Far more than a human friend, God can give you what you truly need.

The psalmist loved God. He was thankful for God's listening ear. He knew he could call upon God at any time. And he would do so as long as he lived.

How about you?

You protect ordinary people, and when I was help-less, you saved me and treated me so kindly that I don't need to worry anymore.

—Psalm 116:6–7

The psalmist offers another reminder of the loving provision and care generously bestowed upon us by the Lord.

In times when the psalmist was helpless, God saved him. And that's a simple truth.

Knowing that God treated him so kindly, and knowing that He would continue to do so, enabled him to relax. He didn't have to worry anymore.

He didn't try to figure it all out. He didn't run his mind through the maze of confusion to find solutions.

He trusted God and put his life into His hands.

What would happen if you did the same?

What must I give you, LORD, for being so good to me? I will pour out an offering of wine to you, and I will pray in your name because you have saved me.

—*Psalm 116:12–13*

Take time to enumerate some of the things God has done for you.

The psalmist did. And lost count. It was an experience that prompted him to ask, How could I ever repay God for all He has done for me? What could I give Him to thank Him for all the good things He has lavished upon me?

It's a natural response. You want to pay back the good done to you.

The problem is, you could never give God anything that would approach what He has given for you.

The psalmist's solution was to take up the drink offering of thanksgiving and continue to pray in God's name.

That's all you can do: Thank Him, and keep trusting Him. Nothing else really matters.

Precious in the sight of the LORD Is the death of His saints.

—Psalm 116:15 NKJV

When someone you love dies, the pain can be overwhelming. The loss is too deep for words. The emptiness can seem bottomless.

When you read this verse, you can gain some measure of comfort. It sounds as though the Lord enjoys it when His children die. But that seems unfair. They may enter into His presence, but they have certainly left yours.

So the words may cut deeper. Because the loss of your loved one isn't precious to you.

But the word *precious* has a different connotation. It's "costly." When a believer dies, it is indeed a loss. And God recognizes it.

You see, God knows your pain, your grief. He knows you have lost much. Even though that precious soul is now with Him in eternity, He grieves with you.

The LORD is on my side, and I am not afraid of what others can do to me.

—*Psalm 118:6*

This bold declaration can give you strength and hope, and it can help you overcome fear.

The Lord is with you. He is at your side. He is within you. And when you realize that, you can bring fear under control. After all, if the almighty Lord of the universe is with you, what can a human do to you?

So when you face conflict or danger, remind yourself of this truth.

But be careful. Don't let the fact that the Lord is on your side encourage you to be divisive or take sides. God is on everyone's side, in some sense.

Of course, He opposes all that is evil. But all of us are sinners.

God doesn't take sides. He *is* truth. So come to *His* side. He will meet you and delight to be with you.

And so my life is safe, and I will live to tell what the LORD has done. He punished me terribly, but he did not let death lay its hands on me.

—Psalm 118:17–18

Sin brings its consequences. Rebellion from God's ways draws His discipline.

The psalmist recognized that. Because of his sin, God punished him. He knew that, he expected it, he struggled through it, knowing its purpose and trusting in the One who sent it.

He also knew that God wouldn't go too far. He wouldn't die; he would live. And living, he would be able and willing to declare what God had done to him and in him.

You may be struggling with some consequences of your sin. It may even be a sin committed long ago, before you walked closely with God. Often the consequences are natural and unavoidable. Know that God has you in the palm of His hand and locked in His loving gaze. Learn what you can from your circumstances, and don't resist them.

This day belongs to the LORD! Let's celebrate and be glad today.

—Psalm 118:24

To start your day, open your eyes. Breathe deeply several times. Then say this prayer. Sing it if you know a tune that goes with it.

Most of all, mean the words. Acknowledge that God has created this day, and set it before you. He will give you everything you need today—food, clothing, shelter. He will give you the emotional support you need—through a friend, your family, or some unexpected source. He will give you the spiritual insight you need—through His Word, through prayer, through a brother or sister or spiritual leader.

He will take care of you in this day. And knowing that enables you to be glad in the day. Even if it's a hard day at work. Or your car falls apart. Or the kids are hard to handle. Even in tough circumstances, you can still trust God that His day is unfolding as it should. And you can rejoice.

God is the LORD, and He has given us light; Bind
the sacrifice with cords to the horns of the altar.

—Psalm 118:27 NKJV

Worship can be reduced to the concept of acknowledging God as Lord, accepting the light
He has given us to live, and responding to His
grace and love with obedience.

The psalmist was worshiping God. And in the
process, he followed the Lord's proscribed manner of sacrifice.

However, he called for the sacrifice to be
bound to the altar. God didn't call for that as part
of the ritual. So what did the psalmist mean?

We can only guess. But binding the sacrifice
indicates determination. Offering something to
God with no reservation, no chance of taking it
back.

What do you need to sacrifice today? Is there
something you've given to the Lord, slipped up
on the altar, then taken back? What do you need
to put into God's hands permanently? Work
through that question with Him.

Our LORD, you bless everyone who lives right and obeys your Law. You bless all of those who follow your commands from deep in their hearts.

—*Psalm 119:1–2*

How can you receive blessing from the hand of God?

The answer is simple. And yet it will likely take you a lifetime to put it into practice.

Those who live right and obey Him will be blessed.

They keep His Word before them as a guide. They follow His commands. Their lives are focused, consistent, and transparent. Their life purpose is clear and sure.

It is their overriding goal in life to obey the Lord.

How does that line up with your life purpose? How blessed are you these days?

Young people can live a clean life by obeying your word. I worship you with all my heart. Don't let me walk away from your commands.

—Psalm 119:9–10

When we're young, we can attribute mistakes in judgment, lapses of self-control, rebellious outbursts, and irrational actions to our tender age. When we become more mature, we don't have that convenient excuse.

The truth is, we're always young in relation to where we'd like to be in our wisdom and growth. As long as we walk this earth, we'll always have to work to lead "a clean life."

How do we do it? By listening to God. Reading His Word. And heeding what we hear. By seeking Him wholeheartedly, yearning for His presence and guidance.

It will always be a challenge: Accept that fact. But a life that's marked by this determination will be clean and free and alive.

I treasure your word above all else; it keeps me from sinning against you.

—Psalm 119:11

God's Word, the Bible, is not a mere book. It is God speaking to us. God opening the door to our minds.

It is living and active and sharper than any two-edged sword, says the writer of the New Testament book of Hebrews.

It is our light, our guide, our way. It is a standing invitation to conversation with God. It is absolute truth, which we can take and filter into our lives by the power of the Spirit.

The psalmist recognized the power of God's Word. He read it, and studied it. He treasured it—thinking through it, memorizing it, meditating on it.

And the more his life was filled with God's truth, the healthier he was. The stronger he was. The cleaner he was.

Today, learn from his example.

I will study your teachings and follow your footsteps. I will take pleasure in your laws and remember your words.

—Psalm 119:15–16

The society in which we live does not encourage us to spend large periods of time in meditation and contemplation. Many of us have bought into the attitude that quiet time is down time. Useless.

You could use that time to be doing something productive. And the more things you do, the better. As a result, life is becoming splintered with activities, and it's hard to build solid relationships—especially with God.

To achieve a thoughtful, deep, supported life through the Scriptures, you need time. Carve out a chunk of time in your schedule in the morning, at midday, or at night. Read a passage thoughtfully. Write down your thoughts.

Keep thinking about it. Mull it over. Argue with it. Listen to God speak to you through His Word. And it will revolutionize your life.

My soul clings to the dust; Revive me according to Your word. . . . My soul melts from heaviness; Strengthen me according to Your word.

—Psalm 119:25, 28 NKJV

When your soul is clinging to the dust, melting from heaviness, as the psalmist puts it, there's only one thing to do. Cry out to God.

Your dead-feeling spirit can be revived. Your weakened soul can be strengthened. And God will use His Word to accomplish it.

When you're feeling low, sometimes the last thing you feel like doing is studying the Bible. But don't look at it that way. Think of it as opening the window to heaven.

Let God's light shine through its pages into your cold heart. Let His warmth rekindle the flames. Let His Word burn its truth into your frozen interior.

Don't deny your feelings; instead, turn them over to the Lord. He will revive and strengthen you, just as He has promised.

I trust [your teachings] so much that I tell them to
kings.

—Psalm 119:46

Why are we sometimes reluctant to speak to
others of the most important relationship in our
lives—our relationship with the God of the universe, who loves us, accepts us, and nurtures us
totally?

Perhaps it's because we've had frightening experiences of attempting to witness to our faith.
Perhaps fear of rejection, humiliation, or getting
in too deep keeps us from making any effort at
all.

Accept those feelings. Acknowledge that it can
be scary to speak to others about something they
may not understand or agree with.

Then put those feelings aside. You know how
strong your relationship is with God; no one can
take it from you; no one can hinder it or inter-
fere with it.

Let God's love flow through you. A simple
word, an act of spontaneous kindness, or a listening ear can open the door to a discussion
about your relationship with the God who loves
you.

My hands also I will lift up to Your commandments,
Which I love, And I will meditate on Your statutes.
—*Psalm 119:48 NKJV*

Lift up your hands. It's an act of worship. A
spontaneous, freeing gesture of praise, honor,
and surrender.

And for the psalmist, it's prompted by the
words of the Lord—His commandments, which
he loves and meditates on.

Is that your reaction when you focus on God's
Word—a free-flowing gift of worship and praise?
It happens only as a result of reading and study.
And of realizing that the Father God who left us
His Word is at work implanting it and nourish-
ing it and growing it in your life. You can also
think of lifting your hands in another sense: ac-
tion. Doing what you read and meditate on.

Worship and obedience: the natural responses
of the child of God who revels in the Word of
God.

Our LORD, your love is seen all over the world. Teach me your laws.

—Psalm 119:64

Your world is continually filled with the grace, acceptance, and love of God. Your growing relationship with God, empowering times of prayer, illuminating meditations on His Word—all speak of His merciful bonds with you. Your supportive friendships, loving family members, all the things that are going right in your life right now—all point to a God who accepts you, forgives you, and showers you with His grace.

Realizing the truth, the psalmist responded with a plea: "Teach me your laws." In other words, as a response to Your love and acceptance, keep me open to Your ways. Show me areas of life where I am unhealthy and need to grow. Open my eyes to behaviors or attitudes that are harmful to myself and to others.

That prayer comes naturally when you realize how full of God's mercy your life really is.

When you corrected me, it did me good because it taught me to study your laws. I would rather obey you than to have a thousand pieces of silver and gold.

—Psalm 119:71–72

The psalmist could see the value in being corrected by the Lord because it forced him to turn to God. It encouraged him to study His Word and find what God would say to him through it.

Without the correction, lethargy would have set in. He would have taken life easier. Taken God's Word for granted. And coasted through life in a daze.

During times of correction, God can truly speak to you through the Bible. You can study His Word with a new perspective.

The psalmist knew the priceless value of God's wisdom—wisdom he could read, study, think through, and work out personally in his life. Even when that life was difficult.

My soul faints for Your salvation, But I hope in Your word. My eyes fail from searching Your word, Saying, "When will You comfort me?"

—*Psalm 119:81–82 NKJV*

The psalmist's soul was so weak from spiritual malnourishment that he felt faint.

He studied God's Word, seeking answers and insights to his difficult circumstances, to the point that his eyes were weary from the search.

He cried out to God, "When will You hear me? When will You be here for me? When will You give me the comfort I so desperately seek?"

Still, through it all, he could say, "I hope in Your word."

As shaken as his life was, his hope remained firm.

He knew God would answer in His time. He could still search, he could still question, but soon, God would be there.

Just as He will be for you.

DAY 316

Nothing is completely perfect, except your teachings.

—*Psalm 119:96*

More than you could ever want or need. More than you could even imagine. Much more than anything else is the Word of God.

The Bible contains a limitless ocean of wisdom and truth and guidance. You could read it and study it for the rest of your life and merely scratch the surface of its treasures.

God's Word is boundless in its perfection, wide enough for any problem you have, deep enough to offer you anything you need. And when it's illuminated by the Spirit and channeled into your life, there is no limit to what you can know or do. The only limit is within yourself.

How deeply have you ventured into the Word? How far out have you swum in it?

It is waiting for you in all its perfect fullness. And in it, God has the answers, the encouragement, the insight you seek.

DAY 317

Your word is a lamp that gives light wherever I walk.
—*Psalm 119:105*

Life can seem so dark at times. Cold, empty, void of good feelings.

The steps ahead of you are shadowed in doubt and confusion. You may feel alone in the darkness, unsure and afraid of what lies ahead of you. You don't know where to turn, which direction to take. In every sense, you are lost. And then the light shines. Because you've turned to God in His Word.

The psalmist proclaims the Word of God as a lamp to show the way ahead. The rocks that threaten, the ruts that could trap you, the forks in the road. And the more aware you are of the light, the brighter it shines for you.

God desires to be your Guide. He desires to take you by your hand and lead you—carry you if need be—on the way ahead. The first step is to open His Book. The second is to pray. The third is to trust.

DAY 318

You are my place of safety and my shield. Your word is my only hope. All of you worthless people, get away from me! I am determined to obey the commands of my God.

—*Psalm 119:114–115*

Life is a constant battle. And the enemies are both within and without.

Inside, you wrestle with fear, lust, anger, envy. You struggle with your emotional exhaustion that keeps you from reaching out for what you need. And unless you realize that battle is being fought within you, you can become increasingly withdrawn, weak, and unhealthy.

Outside, you wrestle with a world at odds with the ways of the Lord. People who use others to further their own interests. People who haven't a clue as to what sacrificial love is or any other foundational truth you've built your life upon.

These battles can drain you of life. Unless you turn to the Lord and see Him as your refuge and as your shield.

I serve you, so let me understand your teachings.
—Psalm 119:125

Surrender. That means to stop working things in your own power, according to your own wisdom, in your own way. That means to come to the end of yourself, recognizing that your strength is as nothing compared to the challenge of life before you. That means to realize you can't do it alone. That means to understand that the freest kind of life comes when you put yourself under bondage to God as His servant.

When you start there, understanding can come. You can receive God's insight without fighting it. And you can accept His abounding love and support.

Pray the psalmist's prayer today. It's the first step toward true freedom of spirit.

Direct my steps by Your word, And let no iniquity
have dominion over me. Redeem me from the oppression of man, That I may keep Your precepts.
—*Psalm 119:133–134 NKJV*

Step by step. That's how we're taking life. The
steps can be light, purposeful, energetic, dancing.
Or they can be painful, slow, heavy, weak, wandering. Or they can be somewhere in between.

How is your walk today? The psalmist offers a
prayer that you can pray.

The psalmist recognizes the difficulties that
iniquity (internal sin) and oppression (external
sin) can place on your walk. Your doubts and
fears can keep you tentative, slow, and wandering. Your pride and arrogance can force you off
the path. Wrongs committed against you can
keep you from moving forward.

Be aware of the forces around you today—the
internal and external forces—that would keep
your steps slow and painful. Turn these forces
over to God. Put yourself under His protection
and guidance. And watch your step.

Even before sunrise, I pray for your help, and I put my hope in what you have said.

—Psalm 119:147

A strained relationship keeps you worrying, thinking, trying to figure out what to do. A financial backstep has you wondering how you'll make it this month and whether it will be worse next month. A rebellious child has you fearful about the consequences of his actions.

Life is full of potential worry zones. And like the psalmist, you've probably spent a sleepless night or two in fear and anxiety over an issue that's important to you.

The psalmist got up before dawn and prayed. He cried to God for help. And through it all, he maintained his hope in God's Word.

You can stop the worry cycle. But you must make a decision of the will to do so. To give it over to God. And keep giving it over to Him whenever you keep taking it back from Him.

I respect your words, because they bring happiness like treasures taken in war. . . . You give peace of mind to all who love your Law. Nothing can make them fall.

—Psalm 119:161–162, 165

How do you feel when you find that wad of cash you hid in your sock drawer for safekeeping and forgot about? Or when you find the diamond that dropped out of your engagement ring? Or when you find the child who got away from you in the shopping mall and wandered out of your sight?

You rejoice. For each is a rich treasure, and finding it brings joy. But God's Word offers so much more.

Unlike any other treasure, it offers peace of mind to those who love and pursue it. Unlike any valuable, the Word of God gives strength, vigor, and energy to live without stumbling in weariness or fear.

Open your spiritual treasure chest today, and dig deep.

I am your servant, but I have wandered away like a lost sheep. Please come after me, because I have not forgotten your teachings.

—Psalm 119:176

Sheep, you may have heard, can be quite stupid. Without guidance and a watchful eye, they are liable to wander away mindlessly and end up in a briar bush or in a ravine.

So when the psalmist says he may stray like a lost sheep, he's not talking about willful disobedience. He's talking about making wrong choices out of ignorance, wandering off the pathway because his mind is elsewhere or his eye has been caught by something afar off.

The psalmist asks God to look for him, to seek him out. After all, he tries to live according to God's will. But he is human.

When you've found you've wandered away from the life God has called you to, ask Him to come after you. And just like a shepherd, He will.

I look to the hills! Where will I find help? It will come from the LORD, who created the heavens and the earth.

—Psalm 121:1–2

The psalmist is on a sojourn. Before him lie the rough, barren hills of his homeland. Hills he must journey through, facing rocky roads, bandits, ruts. Anticipating exhaustion, thirst, hunger.

His path goes forward, toward the hills. What will he encounter? How will his journey go? The prospects build anxiety.

And he acknowledges that he needs help to make his way through the hills.

But where will it come from? Who will meet his needs for courage, strength, and wisdom for the journey? "It will come from the LORD."

Knowing that, he is prepared for his journey. After all, the Lord is the One who made heaven and earth. Which means He made the hills. So if anyone can help him make his way, it's the Lord.

The LORD is your protector, and he won't go to sleep or let you stumble. The protector of Israel doesn't doze or ever get drowsy.

—Psalm 121:3–4

Sometimes God seems distant. Maybe He's angry with us. So He turns His back on us. Or worse, falls asleep listening to our complaints.

No. Never.

God is not like that. The psalmist reminds us that God is constantly aware of our every need. He is continually at work in our lives, whether we feel it or not.

In fact, we can't even slip without His knowing it. And if we are truly walking in His strength, we won't lose our footing anyway.

God doesn't sleep. He doesn't leave His people without protection and care while He catches some sleep. He is ever vigilant, ever watchful, ever aware of you. Your hurts, your emotions, your needs, your fears.

DAY 326

The LORD will protect you and keep you safe from all dangers. The LORD will protect you now and always wherever you go.

—Psalm 121:7–8

The psalmist, on his pilgrimage to the temple, puts his trust in the God who watches and cares for him.

Not only on this journey to the house of God, but on his entire life journey, he knows and trusts God to preserve him.

He is safe "from all dangers." No temptation can cause him to lose his eternal relationship with God.

Every step is protected. Now and forever.

It may feel as though the evil of the world is winning, that its oppression is smothering you spiritually and perhaps even physically. But it won't succeed. Your soul is surrounded by the forces of the almighty God. And He will never, never give in.

Servants look to their master, but we will look to you, until you have mercy on us.

—*Psalm 123:2*

To our minds, the concept of servanthood can be an anathema. Particularly if we liken it to the sordid slavery of America's past.

And yet in the psalmist's time, servants often were loyal, responsive, and thankful for their role. Because they were well treated, often becoming like family members.

The psalmist had this picture in mind regarding the believer's relationship with God.

A servant was ready and eager to serve, watching the hand of the master for any signal. Waiting patiently for the master to respond.

In the same way, the believer looks to the Lord, watching and waiting for His word, His response, His mercy.

Keep praying. Keep asking. Keep waiting for God to respond.

He will. Because He loves His children who wait as His servants to do His will.

Please have mercy, LORD! We have been insulted more than we can stand, and we can't take more abuse from those proud, conceited people.

—Psalm 123:3–4

The people of God had reached their limit. They could take no more.

The proud and scornful people around them—people who did not know God or believe in Him—had ridiculed them and poured out contempt upon them.

And the burden was becoming too heavy to bear.

But rather than lash out against their enemies, rather than return evil for evil, rather than adopt the ways of the enemy in their own defense, they turned to God, crying, "Have mercy, LORD!"

Only God could give them peace.

You may have occasion to make this truth your own today. In the face of ridicule, rejection, or scorn from others, you can react negatively or turn to God. Only one way really works.

Everyone who trusts the LORD is like Mount Zion that cannot be shaken and will stand forever. Just as Jerusalem is protected by mountains on every side, the LORD protects his people by holding them in his arms now and forever.

—Psalm 125:1–2

Think of a time you gazed at a mountain. Perhaps you were on top of one, looking at the neighboring mountains, seeing for miles and miles around you. Perhaps you were at the base, and its craggy height was imposing and awesome to behold.

Do you ever see yourself as a mountain? The psalmist says that everyone who trusts in God is like Mount Zion. Is that a picture you can identify with today?

If not, look at it a different way. With the psalmist, see the mountains surrounding the city of Jerusalem. Realize that's how the Lord surrounds you, now and forever.

You are protected. Strengthened. Secure. You are surrounded by His care and love, encompassed by His mercy and grace.

It seemed like a dream when the LORD brought us back to the city of Zion. We celebrated with laughter and joyful songs. In foreign nations it was said, "The LORD has worked miracles for his people."

—*Psalm 126:1–2*

The people of God, the nation of Israel, had been scattered in judgment for their continual rebellion. Thousands had been taken captive to the land of Babylon. Decades passed. And finally, God moved the heart of the Babylonian king to allow the Israelites to return to their homeland. They were free to go back home.

The joy that broke through in their lives must have been incredible. It was like a dream come true. It was an incredible event, probably unprecedented in history. And the whole world knew it. In fact, the pagan nations admitted that the God of Israel must be powerful. Look what He had done for them!

Next time good news happens, be sure to give credit where it's due.

We cried as we went out to plant our seeds. Now let us celebrate as we bring in the crops. We cried on the way to plant our seeds, but we will celebrate and shout as we bring in the crops.

—Psalm 126:5–6

Sowing is hard work. It can break your back. The muscles can scream in agony.

But the psalmist declares that sowing is a process that—though difficult—will bring about joy. Because a crop results.

Your life involves a great deal of sowing. You're sowing seeds of love, trust, and health every day. You're working to keep your marriage going and growing. You're working to parent your children positively. You're working to be all you can be for God.

It can be painful. It can cause great weeping. But there will be an end. Those who honestly work hard at sowing will celebrate. Why? Because the fruit of your work will fill your life. You'll be bringing in the crops.

Without the help of the LORD it is useless to build a home or to guard a city.

—Psalm 127:1

Life apart from God is meaningless.

Creating anything without God behind it is emptiness.

Building a family, a community, a nation, apart from the living Lord will bring only futility.

Keeping watch over a city is a waste of time if God also isn't guarding it.

What are you doing with your life today?

Where is your career going? How are you raising your family? What relationships are you pursuing and building? What ministries are you involved in?

Without God, it's all just a waste of time and effort.

But with God, you can build mansions. Change lives. Make a difference. Affect eternity.

What a difference! What a God!

DAY 333

It is useless to get up early and stay up late in order to earn a living. God takes care of his own, even while they sleep.

—Psalm 127:2

Workaholism is a disease that's affecting increasing numbers of people today.

They get up early, stay up late, and work bitterly hard to get ahead. And in the wake of their busy lives, they can leave spouses, children, friends—and even God.

The psalmist calls it what it is: "useless."

What's the point? Personal advancement? Financial success? Selfish pride?

Not that hard work is wrong. But hard work to an extreme, without God's power and guidance, is wrong. Because it's harmful.

God gives His beloved sleep. That's a restful thought. We sleep for a God-given purpose: to make us sharper and clearer, more efficient and effective, more energetic and open. Overwork short-circuits God's process.

Today, take time to evaluate your work. You may need a nap.

With all my heart, I am waiting, LORD, for you! I trust your promises. I wait for you more eagerly than a soldier on guard duty waits for the dawn.

—Psalm 130:5–6

A guard on duty does little else but watch. And wait. And wait. Until the morning comes. He watches the horizon intensely for the dawn, so he can go home.

But even more than that guard, the psalmist says he waits for the Lord.

Watching, expecting, praying, hoping.

Every fiber of his being is tuned toward the Lord. He meditates on and hopes in the Word of God. He prays intensely about the concerns on his heart. He waits on the Lord.

How patient are you when it comes to waiting for God to answer your prayer? If you've prayed about it, trust that He heard you and is answering in His perfect time in His perfect way. Wait. And hope.

I am not conceited, LORD, and I don't waste my time on impossible schemes.

—Psalm 131:1

Do you know your limits? Or do you keep frustrating yourself by expecting perfect knowledge and infinite wisdom?

The psalmist admitted that some things were impossible for him.

As a result, he wasn't conceited. He hadn't figured it all out. He wasn't an expert in anything. Except perhaps trusting in God.

There was one thing the psalmist knew: Everything is in God's hands. And God knows it all. And since God is the psalmist's God, that's all he needed to know.

Have you accepted the fact that you'll never fully figure out this life in this life? Are you aware that truth is bigger than your mind could ever hold? Do you really trust the God who is all and in all and knows all? That's how you stay humble.

Surely I have calmed and quieted my soul, Like a weaned child with his mother; Like a weaned child is my soul within me.

—*Psalm 131:2 NKJV*

An infant is one of the most self-absorbed creatures on earth. When he is hungry, he must have mother's milk. He demands it. But as the infant grows and becomes more mature, his self-centered demands are not quite as harsh.

The psalmist understood that in his own life. Rather than demand to be fed, he was content to be held in his mother's arms. He rested in the trust that had been established.

That was the state of his soul with God. He was content to be in God's arms. In quiet confidence, his soul rested in His peace.

He was growing but still a child. And that childlike humility is what God calls for each of us to display.

Behold, how good and how pleasant it is For brethren to dwell together in unity!

—Psalm 133:1 NKJV

For a parent, few things are more frustrating than squabbling siblings.

For an employer, disgruntled employees can cause ulcers.

For a pastor, church factions can cause a crisis of faith.

For a national leader, opposing views can be downright nerve shattering.

But once in a while, you can catch a glimpse of the peace of the kingdom in your home, at work, in your neighborhood, even in the world. And it's like a breath of fresh air.

The psalmist exulted in the pleasantness of the peace of camaraderie and unity.

Unity doesn't mean that everyone thinks alike or acts alike or looks alike. Far from it. It does mean accepting others, loving others for who they are. Giving them room to be what God has made them to be. Working together with various gifts and abilities to create and produce good.

He does as he chooses in heaven and on earth and
deep in the sea.

—Psalm 135:6

God is sovereign. He is all-powerful. He is
able.

As God, He has the authority to rule over His
creation as He sees fit. And this is what the
psalmist reminds us. God does what He pleases
in the totality of creation: the heavens, the earth,
the seas—everywhere.

You may feel lost in the vast expanse of creation. You may think of God as sovereign over
the universe but hardly over your seemingly out-
of-control life. You may feel that He doesn't care
about the minute details of your pain and problems.

But He is sovereign, and He does care. And
He does what He pleases.

If you can trust that fact, the pieces fall into
place. Acceptance comes. And strength from the
acceptance. Your trust in God builds in the
process of accepting.

Praise the LORD! He is good. God's love never fails.
Praise the God of all gods. God's love never fails.

—Psalm 136:1–2

This psalm is a litany for the people's worship of the God they loved.

Every statement about God elicits a strong response: His "love never fails."

Because they knew that to be true, they were thankful for His consummate goodness. And for His absolute power and authority.

Today, think about the ways God has extended His love to you. In forgiveness for your sins. In saving your soul for His eternal pleasure and joy. In building a relationship with you that gives you strength and security. In bringing other brothers and sisters into your life for encouragement, support, and fun. In providing your needs for food, clothing, and shelter. In giving you a glorious planet to enjoy and care for. In reminding you in little ways of His love and care. In hearing and answering your prayers. In lifting your heart in worship and song. Keep the list going.

Only God works great miracles. . . . With wisdom he made the sky. . . . The Lord stretched the earth over the ocean. God's love never fails.

—Psalm 136:4–6

Consider the works of the hands of God. Look into the night sky and be dazzled. See nature's bright, colorful, and complex majesty. Gaze into the eyes of someone you love.

Look beyond all that surface stuff and see what lies behind it all: God's love.

In love, God exploded with endless creativity. There are no limits to what He has accomplished. It is awesome to behold.

Take it all in today. See it for what it is: the divine expression of God's loving mercy toward us.

Learn to look behind what you see, and find a delighted, creative, powerful God who loves you and has given you so much to enjoy in life.

And give thanks.

Beside the rivers of Babylon we thought about Jerusalem, and we sat down and cried. We hung our small harps on the willow trees.

—Psalm 137:1–2

Imagine being forced from your home, from your country, and taken to a distant land, an entirely different culture—one that knew not the God you worshiped.

The psalmist remembered those days in foreign Babylon. When they thought about their homeland, they wept. Their hearts could not sing; their harps were put away. They could only mourn.

Perhaps an event in your life comes to mind. A time you had to move away against your will. The loss of a loved one. A period of depression and mourning. The death of a dream.

Perhaps you're still right in the middle of it. If so, God is there with you. Eventually, God brought His people to triumph over the situation and return to their homeland. He will do the same for you, one way or another.

Here in a foreign land, how can we sing about the LORD?

—Psalm 137:4

When the exiles were in Babylon, they pined to return home. Their lives were on hold; nothing made much sense, their faith was fading, and joy had departed from their lives.

They couldn't make themselves go through the motions of their religion. They were numb with grief, their lives totally displaced and off center. So singing about the Lord would only make the hurt deeper.

You may be in your house today, but you feel as though you're in a foreign land. Life isn't working right. Growth is stalled. God is distant. Setbacks have gotten the best of you.

If that's how you feel, God understands. He knows what's going on in your life. He is waiting for you to come back to your homeland, and you will in your own time. You may not feel it, and you certainly can't sing to Him, but He is with you even now.

With all my heart I praise you, LORD. In the presence of angels I sing your praises. I worship at your holy temple and praise you for your love and your faithfulness. You were true to your word and made yourself more famous than ever before.

—Psalm 138:1–2

Wholehearted praise. Focusing your whole being on God. Praising Him for His love and faithfulness.

Are you that focused when you worship God? Are you able to let go of the emotions, the problems, the circumstances that bind you, and give them over to Him? Can you consider the Lord objectively, and let His light shine on your situation?

Sometimes you can; other times you can't. If you're having difficulty admiring God for who He is, say these verses out loud. Let go of the pain and fear, and the love will remain. He will delight in your wholehearted worship.

Though you are above us all, you care for humble people, and you keep a close watch on everyone who is proud.

—Psalm 138:6

This is the beautiful thing about our relationship with God. He is above us, in heaven, reigning over all of creation, yet He cares for "humble people."

He sees us, knows us, and acts on our behalf—even with everything else that He's responsible for. And yet that happens only when our attitude is humble and accepting.

David notes that God closely watches the proud. He desires to have a relationship with them, but they are not open to the idea. *They* are in control of their lives. And proud of it.

If you sense distance in your relationship with God, examine your heart. If you're bulldozing through life in your own power, He is unwilling to break through to you with His own. Until you recognize your need for Him, you cannot experience Him. But when you do, He is more than willing to meet you where you are.

DAY 345

You have looked deep into my heart, LORD, and you know all about me. You know when I am resting or when I am working, and from heaven you discover my thoughts. You notice everything I do and everywhere I go.

—Psalm 139:1–3

Sometimes it seems impossible to understand ourselves. Why do we do the things we do, think the things we think, feel the things we feel? Some of us accept the unanswered questions and move on; others continue to search and search.

But the answers can be found only in God. And as David reminds us, He knows them well. Because He has searched deep within us. He knows every act, thought, and feeling of our lives.

We can rest in His knowledge and understanding of us. Not that we shouldn't question and search. That effort leads to healthy growth. But we need not agonize over it. We have all the answers we need right now in God.

DECEMBER 10

DAY 346

Before I even speak a word, you know what I will
say, and with your powerful arm you protect me
from every side.

—Psalm 139:4–5

David marvels at God's total knowledge of
him. Rather than feeling invasive or confining or
threatening to him, it is a source of strength and
self-acceptance.

God knows him inside out. Every word he
speaks; every thought he thinks. God surrounds
his soul to protect and nurture; His arm is
around him for comfort and guidance.

The realization boggles David's mind. It's
more than he can understand; it fills him with
wonder and admiration: That God would know
him so intimately and completely—and want to
know him so—seems too good to be true.

And yet it is true. And it fills David with hope
and serenity and strength to face his life.

You, too, can have that hope and serenity and
strength.

DECEMBER 11

Where could I go to escape from your Spirit or from your sight?

—Psalm 139:7

God pursues us. His love and care are relentless. And sometimes that fact overwhelms us.

We may feel like running and hiding, but we can't. David asks rhetorically, "Where could I go to escape?" The answer—so obvious that he doesn't state it directly—is nowhere.

He could go up the heavens, but God would be there. He could travel to a distant land, yet God's hand would be there to guide him.

You can react to that with a feeling of being stifled and restrained, or you can accept it as reality—and come to grips with God's unstoppable love for you.

Do you really want to flee from God's presence or from your own failures and needs? You know the answer to that, deep down. So you can take comfort in God's ever-present Spirit.

DAY 348

I praise you because of the wonderful way you created me. Everything you do is marvelous! Of this I
have no doubt.

—Psalm 139:14

You are a complex creation. You will never be
able to reach the depths of your existence, fully
understand yourself. Physically, your body is a
marvel of efficiency, fascinating in its detail.
Emotionally, you are full of rich texture and
color and depth. Spiritually, there are no limits to
what you can experience with God.

God has made you to be so. He delighted to
put your cells together the way He did. You are
the only person like you; no one else has your
physical, emotional, and spiritual makeup. And
that's a matter of rejoicing.

With God, you can explore and grow and mature, becoming all that He intended you to be.
How well does your soul know that? How accepting of yourself are you?

How freely and genuinely can you praise God
for what He has done?

DECEMBER 13

With your own eyes you saw my body being formed. Even before I was born, you had written in your book everything I would do.

—Psalm 139:16

God takes human cells and forms them into living, breathing creatures capable of carrying His Spirit.

David the psalmist was struck by the intimacy of God's knowledge of him, even while he was being formed in his mother's womb. God saw him, knew him, loved him.

Even before David was born, God knew what would happen every day that he would live. And He loved David despite that knowledge. For God knew David would commit adultery, murder, and assorted other sins. Yet He also knew that David's human heart would pursue God despite—or perhaps because of—his human weaknesses.

God knows you, too. He has known you since the time you were in your mother's womb. He knows what lies ahead for you. And still He loves you. Take joy in that awesome knowledge today.

Your thoughts are far beyond my understanding, much more than I could ever imagine. I try to count your thoughts, but they outnumber the grains of sand on the beach. And when I awake, I will find you nearby.

—Psalm 139:17–18

Have you ever stopped to think how much God thinks of you? How often you cross his mind?

The psalmist did. And the realization was precious to him because it underscored yet again how faithful and loving God is toward His children. Including you.

David figured that the number of times God thought of him was beyond calculation.

And it didn't matter if he was awake or asleep. God was always with him, always thinking of him, always looking out for him.

Why would God do this? Because He can, yes. But also because He wants to. Because He loves each of us. The truth is, you never leave God's mind. You are always on His heart.

Look deep into my heart, God, and find out everything I am thinking. Don't let me follow evil ways,
but lead me in the way that time has proven true.

—Psalm 139:23–24

Do you dare to make this prayer of David your
own today?

Are you willing to stand utterly naked before
the God of the universe without defense, without
subterfuge, without excuse?

Are you willing to open your heart to Him, al-
lowing Him to examine you, test your thoughts
and feelings, know your anxieties?

Are you willing to put yourself totally into His
hands and let Him lead you on the path He has
set before you—a path that leads to eternity with
Him?

He already knows you and everything about
you. Cooperating in the process only hastens it,
embellishes it, and fulfills it. Allow Him to work
in wondrous ways within you.

Rescue me from cruel and violent enemies, LORD!
They think up evil plans and always cause trouble.

—*Psalm 140:1–2*

Your environment can make all the difference
in the world. Dwell in darkness, and you will
tend to be dark-minded. Associate with evil, and
the evil will spread like a virus attacking your system. Live exposed to violence, and you will likely
get hurt.

So David prayed that the Lord would deliver
him from such an environment and protect him
from evil and violence.

In this world, surprise attacks are possible—
and even probable. It is wise to be on guard. And
God is more than willing to surround you with
His protection.

Evil will always be at work in this world until
the end of the age. The wise child of God is prepared to deal with it when it rears its ugly head—
but only in God's power.

Are you prepared? Dwell in the light. Associate with good. Live exposed to the transforming
Spirit of God. And He will deliver you.

Our LORD, I know that you defend the homeless and see that the poor are given justice. Your people will praise you and will live with you because they do right.

—Psalm 140:12–13

I know."

How many times do you say these words every day? How casually do you utter them? They can become a prideful boast, a caustic put-down, an irritated gesture of dismissal.

How often do you mean them as David does here—in the sense of unshakable confidence? Of absolute trust in the Lord of your life? Of unyielding faith that He will do what He has promised to do?

David expresses his confidence that God will always act consistently with His character—lovingly, caringly, givingly, justly. He will protect those who are oppressed. And in one way or another, that's all of us.

As a result, the children of God will live thankfully, uprightly, and honestly in His presence. But only if they *know* it.

DAY 354

Help me to guard my words whenever I say something. Don't let me want to do evil or waste my time doing wrong with wicked people. Don't let me even taste the good things they offer.

—Psalm 141:3–4

You're under pressure. You're about to explode with hurtful remarks, angry rebukes. You feel vulnerable. Your guard is down. And before you know it, you find yourself acting out a behavior you had no idea you would ever do. How do you respond to your wandering soul?

Here is a prayer of David that would make an excellent start. Help me control what I say and how I say it, in the most healthy way possible. Keep my heart holy, inclined toward You, God. Keep my eyes focused on You and not on the temptation.

Pray ahead. Then when the temptation to say or do something you know is harmful arises, you'll have the power to conquer the urges.

I remember to think about the many things you did in years gone by. Then I lift my hands in prayer, because my soul is a desert, thirsty for water from you.
—*Psalm 143:5–6*

David found himself in a tight spot. And he brought to mind the many times in his past that God had acted on his behalf. He thought about the works God had performed so mightily in his life.

God had done it for him in the past. He could do it for him now. So he humbled himself before the Lord and asked one more time for help.

God never tires of hearing our prayers or of answering them. When we are needy, overwhelmed, dying inside, He stands ready to provide whatever we need, surround us with His loving protection, and refresh us with new life in the Spirit.

Remember how God has worked in you and through you in the past? Today, create a new memory of His mighty provision. Ask for it.

Each morning let me learn more about your love because I trust you. I come to you in prayer, asking for your guidance.

—*Psalm 143:8*

How do you begin your day? Your eyes open sleepily. Then your mind starts working through the day ahead.

The meeting with the client you've had such trouble pleasing. Your child's cold that just won't go away. The funny noise your car is making. The bills you need to pay before you get your next paycheck. On and on it goes, until your stomach gets tied up in knots, and you just want to cover your head with your blanket and make it all go away.

Here's another option. Don't deny that these things are real in your life, but pray through them. As soon as you can make a conscious thought, tell yourself, This is the day the Lord has made—I will rejoice and be glad in it. Then pray about all the things as they come to your mind. Turn them over to God. And He will guide you through the day.

Why do we humans mean anything to you, our
LORD? Why do you care about us? We disappear like
a breath; we last no longer than a faint shadow.

—Psalm 144:3–4

Feeling small. Unimportant. Unworthy of notice. And certainly beneath the gaze of almighty
God. Why does God even care? Why does our
insignificant existence matter to Him at all?
We're barely an iota in the universe, and He
knows us?

Our lives are so brief—like a breath or a
shadow. Inconsequential.

Do your thoughts turn in this direction? You
may become so overwhelmed by the majesty and
infinity of God that you feel insignificant. David
did, and he expressed his feelings here.

And yet, that's the beautiful part of our relationship with God. Yes, He is majestic. Yes, He is
infinite in His power and knowledge and being.
And even so—*even so*—He knows us. Loves us.
Cares for us. And keeps us with Him forever and
ever.

Won't you keep me safe from those lying foreigners who can't tell the truth? Let's pray that our young sons will grow like strong plants and that our daughters will be as lovely as columns in the corner of a palace.

—Psalm 144:11–12

David's prayer is not one of prejudice against persons; it's against paganism. In his day, the nations around Israel were brutal in their worship of false idols. Since the gods they worshiped were nonexistent, their words were useless, their actions false. David asked God to keep him out of their influence.

Our world is filled with idolatries. Rarely are they gods carved in stone or precious metals, but they are idols nonetheless. And they are false.

Only when we keep our hearts pure and our minds open to God alone can we raise sons and daughters who have a foundation to grow on, and strength and stamina for their own journeys. So they can stand tall as stately columns and healthy trees.

I will extol You, my God, O King; And I will bless
Your name forever and ever. Every day I will bless
You, And I will praise Your name forever and ever.
Great is the LORD, and greatly to be praised; And
His greatness is unsearchable.

—*Psalm 145:1–3 NKJV*

Great. Today you'll hear that word in conversations, advertisements, television programs, and
many other places. It will be applied to breakfast
cereals, movies, emotional states, and politicians.
You'll probably say it at least a few times yourself.
And like many words in our language, its overuse
has made it empty of meaning.

But David uses it in three forms in one passage, referring to God: "Great is the LORD, and
greatly to be praised; And His greatness is unsearchable."

As he worships, he gets carried away in the
majesty of God. He is great in that He is infinite,
above all, absolutely distinguished from all else.
And because He is great, He greatly deserves our
deepest, highest, biggest worship.

You are merciful, LORD! You are kind and patient and always loving. You are good to everyone, and you take care of all your creation.

—Psalm 145:8–9

Sometimes we get unbalanced in our understanding of God as the Judge, the holy One who will not tolerate sin, who decimates wickedness in the end, who rules from on high. That's a true picture. And worthy of keeping in mind.

But today, you may need to remind yourself of your place in His heart. His goodness toward you. His tender mercies extended to you—and to all—without hesitation or holding back.

Thank God that He is slow to anger. He does get angry—perfectly, righteously so. But He gives us all the patience and forbearance we need as human beings. And while He is slow to anger, He is also great in mercy, "always loving," offering an inexhaustible abundance of grace that's far more than we could ever, ever hope to deserve.

He will fulfill the desire of those who fear Him; He also will hear their cry and save them. The LORD preserves all who love Him, But all the wicked He will destroy.

—Psalm 145:19–20 NKJV

Fear and love—two ways of looking at the same relationship with God.

You fear Him by acknowledging His all-encompassing power, His ultimate judgment, His unyielding authority.

You love Him by experiencing His love, mercy, grace, and provision for you.

Both aspects are present in a balanced relationship with God.

For those who fear and love Him, He fulfills their desire for more of Him in their lives. He hears their prayers of joy and frustration, of praise and pain. And He saves them—He preserves those who are in right relationship with Him forever.

Take a look at your relationship with God. Keep yourself in balance. God is worthy of both fear and love.

Happy is he who has the God of Jacob for his help, Whose hope is in the LORD his God, Who made heaven and earth, The sea, and all that is in them; Who keeps truth forever.

—Psalm 146:5–6 NKJV

The pursuit of happiness. America was founded, in part, on that principle. And our society exemplifies a culture gone amok in the pursuit of happiness.

But what is happiness? A state of blissful euphoria? Getting everything you want? Success? A high? Or is true happiness something else entirely?

The psalmist would argue for the latter. He declares that happiness is found only when you trust and hope in the Lord your God.

If you truly focus your life on following after God, you will experience a joy that forms a foundation of all kinds of emotions. Life in all its splendor is played out on that foundation. And though you may be sad or angry or bored or ecstatic, the joy of the Lord remains.

[The LORD] heals blind eyes. He gives a helping hand to everyone who falls. The LORD loves good people and looks after strangers. He defends the rights of orphans and widows, but destroys the wicked.

—Psalm 146:8–9

God is active in His love for His needy children. He plays out His affections openly. He works at providing everything we need.

He "heals . . . gives . . . loves . . . looks after . . . defends." His is an energetic love.

So if you're blind—physically, spiritually, emotionally—He can heal your eyes. If you've fallen—in humiliation, pain, or depression—He can lift you up. If you're lonely and in a strange place, He can watch over you and protect you. If you're seeking the love of a lost parent or spouse, He can give it to you in abundance. He can do all that and more, no matter what your need may be.

What is your need today? Ask Him to meet it—and watch Him go to work.

Shout praises to the LORD! Shout the LORD's praises in the highest heavens. All of you angels, and all who serve him above, come and offer praise. Sun and moon, and all of you bright stars, come and offer praise. Highest heavens, and the water above the highest heavens, come and offer praise.

—*Psalm 148:1–4*

Imagine the joyful cacophony of heaven! The endless songs of praise of all angelic beings. The unstoppable music of the stars and planets and moons. The unrelenting joy of worship for the Lord, the Creator, the Sustainer.

Can you hear it? It will always be there. And someday, you'll be part of it.

Today, take a moment to stop, close your eyes, and focus on God. Imagine this passage being played out right in front of your eyes. Hear the music!

Soon, you'll find yourself invited to join in. Your heart lifted in praise. Sing! He is worthy. And all creation acknowledges that. Will you?

Shout praises to the LORD! Sing him a new song of praise when his loyal people meet. People of Israel, rejoice because of your Creator. People of Zion, celebrate because of your King.

—Psalm 149:1–2

The psalmist leads the nation of Israel in a song of praise to God, who has given them victory over their enemy.

He can lead you today as well to praise, sing, rejoice, and celebrate, for God has done the same for you.

"Sing a new song!" the psalmist urges us. And that prods our hearts and minds. For God our Creator has given us a sense of creativity, a desire for newness and freshness.

He deserves the best you can give Him when you praise. Certainly, you have favorite praise songs you enjoy singing over and over. But try something new today. He is worthy of creativity in worship.

Shout praises to the LORD! Praise God in his temple. Praise him in heaven, his mighty fortress. Praise our God! His deeds are wonderful, too marvelous to describe. . . . Let every living creature praise the LORD. Shout praises to the LORD!

—Psalm 150:1–2, 6

Here is the doxology for the book of Psalms, a triumph of praise and adoration.

It's a song imbued with energy and fervor, heartfelt devotion and absolute surrender.

It's a song that can lead you to higher levels of praise for the God who dwells on high, the God who invites you into His presence.

It's a song whose spirit can remain with you throughout your day—at work and at home, in crisis and conflict, in pain and sadness, in victory and joy.

It's a song that doesn't deny the pain of human existence but enables you to carry all that baggage into the heavenlies and drop it at His feet.

It's a song you can sing today and every day. As long as you have breath to sing it.

SUBJECT INDEX